MIDNIGHT RETURN

Also by Billy Hayes:

Midnight Express

The Midnight Express Letters:
From a Turkish Prison 1970–1975

MIDNIGHT
RETURN

ESCAPING MIDNIGHT EXPRESS

To Paul / Thanks /

BILLY HAYES

CBP

Permissions and Credits
The author gratefully acknowledges permission to include here the following letters (or portions of) written to him by "Harvey Bell" [listed by date]: 12-74 (page 14), 9-75 (page 43), 1-76 (page 95), 4-4-78 (page 137-138), early 1978 (page 139), 10-2-78 (page 152-154), 2-29-79 (page 162), 3-17-79 (page 162-163), 5-12-80 (page 165-166), 5-18-80 (page 167), 6-10-80 (page 167-168), 7-19-80 (page 168-169), 8-8-80 (page 174-175), 12-1-80 (page 190).

Photos:
Pages 2, 3, 128, 132 - *Midnight Express*, © 1978 Columbia Pictures Industries, Inc., All Rights Reserved. Courtesy of Columbia Pictures.
Page 80 - Photo by Harry Benson. All Rights Reserved.
Page 87 - Courtesy of Barbara Belmont.
Page 136 - Courtesy of Eric Morris.
Page 141 - Courtesy of Jill Chastain.

Published by Curly Brains Press
3520 Overland Ave., Suite A157
Los Angeles, CA 90034
curlybrainspress@gmail.com

ISBN: 978-0-9889814-5-4

Cover design and author photo: ad@centrum.is
Cover photo copyright © Grant Faint (www.grantfaint.com)
Interior design and layout by Lee Lewis Walsh, Words Plus Design (www.wordsplusdesign.com)

For Wendy and her true heart.

ACKNOWLEDGMENTS

To my teachers in all their forms, each a uniquely wondrous strand in the tapestry of my life, I send thanks and gratitude.

In writing about my friend Harvey Bell's ongoing trials and tribulations in prison after my escape, I was fortunate to have firsthand knowledge of many of the people and places around him. I was also able to speak with him and reference his own compelling letters, some of which are printed here. When Harvey read an early version of this book he wished me well with it; for himself, he mostly preferred to forget. We talk now and then, he plays his guitar less now but enjoys it more, and the world keeps rollin' round...

CONTENTS

LIST OF ILLUSTRATIONS

1

Madness and Magic

On a warm May night in Cannes, 1978, thunderous applause echoed off the ornate walls of the Palais des Festival. The crowd of tuxedoed men and elegant women rose to its feet, cheering and crying, as the last credits flickered across the screen and the huge chandeliers suddenly blazed with light. We'd done it! At the most prestigious film festival in the world, and before a normally jaded audience, *Midnight Express* was a triumphant success.

I was an emotional wreck. I huddled down in my seat, sweating and totally drained, unable to control the tears. My five years of prison life had just been portrayed on the screen. For two hours I'd sat trapped between the images before me and the memories behind me. I wanted to crawl under the seat and hide, but hands were hauling me up beside the actors, producers and director. I clung to the balcony railing as hundreds of cameras flashed and waves of applause swept the theatre. It was frightening yet fulfilling to know that the events of my life, through a book and now a film, had touched so many people. The air throbbed with their emotions. I felt directly connected to each person in the room—naked and vulnerable but somehow terribly strong. It was as if the power of the connections threatened to absorb me even as it filled me to bursting.

I was aware of the bitter irony of my situation as I wandered around the after-screening party thrown by Columbia Pictures in the ballroom across from the Palais. I smiled and laughed and accepted the congratulatory words of praise, all the while struggling

to hide the confusion and guilt growing inside me. Rona Barrett, reigning queen of the Hollywood gossip columnists, cornered me for an on-camera interview.

"Must be strange to watch a film about your own life," said Rona.

"That's for sure," I said.

Rona looked at my face. "Looks like it affected you as much as the rest of us. How do you feel?"

"Sort of trapped—between the movie and the memories."

"Well, your family must be so happy to have you home."

"Yeah, it was hard for them," I said, staring down at the floor.

"Not knowing and worrying," said Rona.

"Right."

"Do you feel guilty about that?" asked Rona.

I looked up. "Of course, it was one of the worst things about prison."

She smiled at me. "Well, now it's finished and the worst part is over. You're a hero."

So how come I felt like a hypocrite? We finished and I bolted for the men's room. It was crowded, with all the stalls occupied and strange snuffling sounds obvious even behind the closed doors. I was unzipped at the urinal when a dapper older gentleman sidled up

beside me, glanced down, then gave me a wink. I quickly finished up. As I headed for the door, a smiling black man said something to me in French, shook my hand and casually pressed a vial of cocaine into my palm.

Outside, the party had intensified as more people poured in to share the celebration. Francis Ford Coppola talked shop with director Alan Parker. Producers Peter Guber and David Puttnam were answering questions for the press. I searched for a side exit, desperate to get away and be alone, but was caught in a circling net of exuberant well-wishers. My face kept smiling and my mouth spouted inane little responses while I scurried around in my head, feeling as trapped as when I was in prison. I didn't want to talk to people, I wasn't proud of myself, and I had grave misgivings about the film that was causing all this attention. In prison you avoided attracting attention, it was dangerous. Here I was at the center of it.

I had a quick flash of a baby rat struggling against the string I'd tied to his back leg. I was about to lose control when a young blonde woman with the face of an angel appeared at the edge of the crowd. She looked at me for a moment, her stillness setting her apart from the frenzied group, then moved steadily forward and held out her hand, asking me to dance. I stood there staring, then she stepped even closer and smiled up at me with such a certainty and gentleness in her blue-green eyes that folding her in my arms seemed like the most natural thing in the world.

We moved out onto the dance floor, swaying together with an ease that amazed me. She rested her head against my heart, and as we danced I became aware of a growing bubble that seemed to isolate us from the surrounding madness of the night. I thought about the madness of other nights and marveled at the strange workings of Fate...

2

A Vast Abyss of Pain and Fear

Sagmalcilar prison lay frozen and still, locked in the depths of a frigid November night. A ship wailed somewhere out in the harbor beyond Istanbul, and I carefully drew the file across the iron bar on the toilet window. It screeched like a fingernail on a blackboard.

It was 1974 and I was in my fourth year of a thirty-year sentence for smuggling two kilos of hash. I'd originally been sentenced to four years, but just fifty-four days from release the sky fell on my head when the high court in Ankara re-sentenced me. I was not a happy camper.

The screeching file froze Harvey Bell and me, our breath steaming the air.

Harvey looked around the corner at the huddled bundles of snoring men in the barracks-like cellblock—no one seemed to have heard. I tried to move the file slower, with heavy pressure. Harvey nervously coiled the nylon rope on his shoulder, his skinny body shivering beneath a cheap cloth coat. This was an insane plan—even if we got out the window and onto the roof, the guards in the towers would probably pick us off like flies—but Harvey and I both had thirty-year prison sentences, so sanity was becoming difficult to define.

Harvey Bell was a grinning wild man from Alabama who'd been caught driving a nifty green TR3 with 200 kilos of hash hidden beneath it. He'd spent three years in a small prison in central Turkey and was transferred to Sagmalcilar after a botched escape attempt had left him beaten, but not broken. He showed up one day and proceeded to turn life there atilt.

"Yeeess!" he'd shouted, as he entered the foreigners' cellblock, a battered guitar in his hand. "Where the hell are the Americans and who's in charge of escape around here? Goddamn, ah'm so tired of fuckin' Turks an' fuckin' Ah-rabs and fuckin' Muslims."

I was the only American in a cellblock full of Arabs and Muslims, so I wasn't thrilled to hear this scruffy madman bellowing about escape. I got closer and realized he'd managed to get himself drunk on the long trip here from Elazig.

"Oh, man, it's clean here," he drawled, a silly smile creasing his thin, ascetic face. I looked around at the dirt and scum, sniffed the putrid smell coming from the toilet, and made a mental note never to transfer to Elazig prison.

I informed him of his situation and advised him to keep his voice down, but the damage had already been done. That evening I had to intervene in a pipe-swinging confrontation between Harvey and a Jordanian car thief who'd taken grave offense to Harv's comments about the Muslims. It wasn't the most auspicious beginning to a relationship, but during the following year we became best friends, and like most guys in prison, spent our days plotting and planning escape attempts that we never carried out. There's a vast abyss of pain and fear between planning an escape and actually trying it.

Harvey, like myself, had been an English major in college, and his gruff exterior hid a sharp, educated mind. We shared the books that passed through the prison, talked philosophy, and argued politics. He was a good ole boy who could quote Faulkner. "Lib Arts degree oughta be good for sumpin," he'd laugh.

I made the mistake of telling Harvey about one escape plan—cut through the bars, climb onto the roof, then slide down the wall with a nylon rope I'd improvised from a volleyball net that had mysteriously disappeared one day after a game. I'd had the file hidden away for several years, a parting gift from Claude LeBrun, a Belgian diamond thief who'd been released. I'd never tried the plan, because the bullet percentage was way too high. Even if we managed to cut the bar without being spotted, the chances of getting down the wall past the machine gun posts were, as Harvey would say, thinner than frog hair split four ways.

But once Harvey heard I had the file and rope, he was unrelenting; and then one cold November afternoon a letter arrived from my mom:

> *November 15, 1974*
> *Billy,*
> *   ...here I am remembering about long ago. They say that's a sign of growing old. I'm fine. Still the same. Life goes on, even with a little heartache every day for my oldest child so far away.*
> *   Love,*
> *   Mom*

The letter devastated me. The pain my mother had to bear because of me hollowed out my heart. I picked up Harvey's old guitar and began to play the few chords I knew. Harvey came by and began to softly sing some old Alabama blues. We found a simple beat and improvised a song that seemed to write itself:

Mmmm...got the blues, babe,
Got those old Istanbul blues.
Said, yeah, I got the blues, babe,
Got those old Istanbul blues,
Thirty years in Turkey, babe,
Ain't got nothin' left to lose.
Busted at the border,
Two keys in my shoes,
Said I was busted at the border,
With two keys in my shoes,
'An they gave me thirty years, babe,
To learn the old Istanbul blues.
I said now Lord save me, save me,

Please save me from this pain.
I said Lord come and save me,
Come save me from this pain.
An' set me free Sweet Jesus,
I won't never sin again...

The song wore down to a stop, then Harvey asked, "How long you been here, Willie?"

He knew the answer. "Four years," I said.

"How many summers?"

"Four."

We sat while he plucked some strings. Then he stopped and looked at me. "Four summers. They're stealing our summers, man. And now here comes another fucking winter. I mean, can you ever get back a lost summer? Can you?"

I must have been crazed at the time, because I agreed to try the roof escape with him that very night, which was why I found myself cutting nervously at a bar in the toilet window, certain the guards would burst in and drag us away.

"C'mon, for Christ's sake," whispered Harvey.

"It's slower than I thought." I filed for a while, fighting the building panic as I realized I'd misjudged the timing.

"You said it'd cut like butter," said Harvey.

"I was wrong."

Harvey worked at it for a while. The bar only had a slight scratch mark. This would take forever.

We worked in shifts, one man filing while the other kept guard. I looked out at the dark sky through the bars. Five a.m. and we'd barely dented the tough metal.

"We'll have to try again tonight," I said.

Harvey stared at me, then coughed and spit on the filthy stone floor. "Fuck it. We try again tonight."

I picked up an old butt and Harvey scraped some putty from the window frame. We mixed the cigarette ashes with the putty and dabbed the mixture on the bars.

"We got lots of time, right?" grinned Harvey.

We both laughed.

Three days later, just before dawn, I woke in fear to the sound of guards rushing into the cellblock. They were led by Arief the Bonebreaker. They made straight for Harvey's bunk, and two guards dragged him up by the arms. He shook them off. Arief slammed him across the face.

"Who else was with you!" Arief bellowed. "Where is the file?"

They dragged Harvey to the bathroom. Arief rubbed away at a few bars until he dislodged the makeshift putty. "They saw you," he said, pointing across at the children's cellblock across the yard. "You and someone else."

Arief backhanded Harvey across the face.

"Where's the file?"

What else could Harvey do? He went to the locker and dug the file out from under the metal molding in the back.

"Who else was with you?" demanded Arief.

Harvey stared into Arief's face.

Arief smiled and told the guards to take Harvey to the cellar. They dragged him past me, and we made flickering eye contact. I kept my face a mask, but my heart slowly filled with fear and anguish as the metal door slammed shut and Harvey's shouts faded away.

The next day I slipped the door guard a couple of packs of cigarettes and bribed my way over to the prison dispensary, where I heard Harvey had been taken.

I entered the dispensary and walked down a row of small cells. Harvey wasn't there. I turned to leave, then looked again at a prisoner lying in bed with a puffy, blackened face.

"Harvey! Jesus Christ! I didn't recognize you."

He roused himself to a sitting position. "Hey, Willie. Yeah, they really fucked me up," he mumbled through swollen lips. "Goddamn Arief kicked me in the balls. Think he opened my hernia."

It hurt me to look at him.

"They wanted my name, didn't they?"

"Yeah."

"Thanks, Harv."

He smiled and winced. "Yeah, well, what could I do?"

"I owe you," I said.

"Listen, Billy, tell the Consul. I'm afraid the Turks are gonna hustle me away to some little prison in the sticks."

"I'll contact him, Harv."

"And do yourself a favor and get the hell out of this prison while you still can. This place is bad news."

I stared at him awhile. "I won't forget you."

"Everybody forgets when they leave here, you know that."

"I owe you."

He nodded.

"Oh, yeah," I said, slipping a few blue Nembutal capsules between the bars, "These might help."

"Thanks," he said, taking them, "but some acid might be better."

I laughed. "This place is definitely a trip."

We stared at each other.

I lifted a string of dark rosary beads with a tiny silver crucifix out of my pocket.

"I want you to have these," I said, flipping them onto his bed.

Harvey picked up the beads, stared at them. "You must be shitting me, you don't believe this crap."

"I know, but my old grandmother sent 'em to me, said they were blessed by the Pope or something, and I want you to have them."

Harvey smiled at me, then winced.

"Go with God," I said, in Turkish.

He smiled again. "Go with God."

Two days later he was gone.

3

From the Frying Pan

Harvey's balls were still swollen when the rattling old red prison van rolled down the long stone ramp into the sunken courtyard of Antakya Ceza Evi. He smiled around his bruised lips at the Turkish phrase *ceva evi*—literally, "house of pain." Nothing could be much more painful than the thirty-six-hour drive from Istanbul, chained in the back of a freezing van as it bounced and rumbled across the frozen Turkish landscape.

The blue bombers had helped, but he was in great pain from the kick in the nuts. This was his second failed escape attempt in three years, and he knew his body couldn't take much more.

The back doors of the van swung open with a glare, and Harv had a brief view of aging granite walls before the soldiers grabbed his chains and hauled him out. He must have passed out, because when he awoke it was nighttime and he was on a cot beneath some coarse blankets. He heard whispered voices and opened his eyes.

He was in a low-ceilinged barracks-like room, and several men in prison pajamas and tattered robes were sitting on the surrounding beds, smoking cigarettes and talking about him in Turkish.

A heavy balding fellow with a sling on his left arm let a slow stream of smoke flow past his droopy moustache and said, "He's all fucked-up now, but he'll be *tatli* ("sweet") when he heals."

"Ayip," said a thin man with a gray beard and a gauze patch over one eye, "that's disgusting talk."

"My apologies, Baba," said Ayip, looking back at Harvey and grinning like a wolf, "but you haven't been in here as long as I have."

"He's just another goddamn hippie," said a ratty fellow with ferocious acne. "I don't care if you fuck him or fuck him up."

This seemed to be the prison dispensary. There were a dozen beds, half that many prisoners. It was relatively warm. Harvey saw ice on the bars beyond the frosted glass windows beside his bunk. With much pain, he managed to pull himself up into a sitting position. Baba motioned for him to lay back down, but Harvey stared at Ayip for a moment then turned and smashed his fist through the window. The men rushed toward him in surprise but stopped abruptly when Harvey grabbed a shard of glass and swung it in a wide arc.

He looked around the circle then said, in Turkish, "Anybody fucks with me, I take their eye out." He slowly dragged the glass down his forearm, a red trail of blood following the movement. The men all gaped at him.

Gotta make a good first impression, thought Harvey, before he passed out again.

4

Sea of Dreams

Six months after our failed escape attempt, my t-shirt clung to my body and fat flies buzzed through the hot oppressive air of the cellblock as I packed the last of my belongings into a battered leather suitcase. There were a couple of letters from Harvey, still in the Antakya prison but trying to get transferred back to Istanbul where the medical attention was better.

He'd told me he'd been visited by Harriet James, a sweet old lady who lived in Adana with her daughter and Turkish son-in-law. She'd ridden hundreds of miles on a rambling bus through the cold, wet rain. She'd brought him cookies, food and a thermos of coffee. He said he was spaced out on the codeine pills the doctor had prescribed to ease the pain in his liver, spleen and kidneys—all those things that don't respond well to hobnailed boots. During the course of the conversation he'd asked her, "By the way, what day is it?"

She'd looked at him with surprise. "Why, it's Christmas," she replied.

He still hadn't gotten over that.

I'd hoped to see him again before I left, but that wasn't going to happen now as the scratchy, high-pitched loudspeaker began announcing names of prisoners to be transferred:

"Jenghis Bokshoy, Ziat Elakbashi..."

I'd arranged a transfer to Imrali Island prison, twenty miles off the Turkish mainland in the Sea of Marmara. I didn't know how, but I'd find a way to escape—I'd be free, or I'd be dead.

13

Hi Willie

Just got a Xmas card from Harriett Jones and I thought I'd pass on her address to you: it's "2730 Stevens, Parsons, KS 67354 Tel 316 421 3482.

Did I ever tell you that when they shipped me down to Antahya, she visited me a couple of times. I was fucked. All that kicking in Istanbul hurt me. Liver, spleen, kidneys — all those things don't respond well to hobnail boots.

One day Harriett left her daughter and son-and-law's home in Adana and boarded a Turkish bus in the cold, wet rain. Hundreds of kilometers. She brought me some cookies and a thermos of coffee. I was spaced-out on codein pills the prison doctor had prescribed for pain. During the course of the conversation I said "By the way, what day is it?" She look surprised. "Why, it's Christmas," she replied.

I still haven't gotten over that.

And apparently I still haven't gotten over these hobnail boots. The second operation they performed to remove this fluid from my right testicle was a failure. These quack doctors have really put me through some shit.

I've requested a transfer to Istanbul and

"Villiam Ha-yes," droned the loudspeaker, "Villiam Ha-yes..."

In the basement of Sagmalcilar prison a burly soldier who smelled of garlic wrapped dull metal chains around my wrists and snugged them tight with a padlock. He led me out to the cobblestone courtyard and into the back of a red prison van. The door slammed shut, he yelled something to the driver, and we jostled out into the narrow, winding streets of Istanbul.

The stony-faced soldier stared at me as I twisted around on the wooden bench and pressed my face against the narrow window slats. Outside, so tantalizingly close, Freedom slid past my hungry eyes. I saw bustling people, hustling merchants, vendors weighing fruit on balance scales, shish kebabs sizzling in stalls and a small boy leading a muzzled bear on a chain.

Then the van stopped abruptly and the door swung open. Bright sunlight bounced off blue water and the Galatae Bridge spanned the busy harbor, where I saw scuttling fishing dinghies, graceful sailboats, and the huge freighters whose booming voices I'd heard drifting through my dreams for so many dark nights now. The soldier led me down towards a small group of chained prisoners loading onto an old metal ferry that creaked gently against the aged wooden dock.

Another soldier grabbed my chains and pulled me onto the boarding ramp. The boat rolled slightly as we stepped on board. The soldier sat me beside a dirty window, and the rocking sensation of the boat flooded me with memories of clam boats and another life on Long Island Sound. I stared out the dirty window of the ferry at the blue wonder of the sea as the spires of Istanbul receded into the distance.

Imrali Island was a small arc of land about twenty miles off the southwestern coast of Asia Minor in the Sea of Marmara. A swift, dark current swept around the island, moving down toward the Dardanelles.

A red sun was dropping into the sea as I stepped from the ferry onto an old stone pier in a small horseshoe-shaped harbor. A little village of crumbling whitewashed buildings lay nestled at the base of rocky shrub-covered hills. I looked up at the rusting metal sign above me—*IMRALI CEZA EVI.*

Several guards lined up the prisoners and marched us off the pier toward the faded buildings glowing softly in the evening light. The soft clattering of our chains mixed with the sound of the waves lapping on the rocky beach. It was really quite beautiful. I took a deep breath and vowed to find a way to escape from here or die trying.

5

Harvey Looks on the Bright Side

Harvey rolled off his bunk, stepped into his rubber Tokyo's and shuffled toward the grungy bathroom at the end of the cellblock. A summer dawn was breaking beyond the bars, a chittering flock of swallows slicing through the opalescent air. Most of the men were still asleep, snoring beneath their sweaty sheets. A brief, muffled sob broke from a large man against the wall, but no one was disturbed. Funny, thought Harvey, how the toughest guys by day often cried in their sleep at night.

Harvey was thankful his hernia was better, but the kicking in Istanbul must have shaken up his plumbing, because he had to piss a lot more than before. It usually got him up before dawn, but he was enjoying the early morning hours before the rest of the prison woke. He shuffled into the bathroom, happy to see that the slick stone around the three holes in the floor was still relatively dry— another advantage to early rising. By noon, the eighty or so men who used this room would have left it wet and slimy.

He loosened his drawstring pajamas and squatted over the center hole, which was set a bit higher than the others. He tried to remember how long it had been since he'd sat on a toilet.

What the fuck, he thought, as piss splattered on the stone, at least my balls don't hurt anymore. Gotta look on the bright side. A rat scuttled out of the corner, clattered across the floor and scurried down the hole beside him. Harvey had to laugh. Right, the bright side.

6

Escape From Imrali Island

Imrali prison was just a handful of old buildings that might have been a village years ago. There were dormitory-style rooms with creaky wooden floors and metal bunk beds. Thirty or so guys to a barracks. It was quaint in a way, if you ignored the guard towers at the mouth of the harbor and the searchlights playing along the beach at night and the sentries patrolling with machine guns. But the atmosphere was different from Sagmalcilar, because most of the guys here were short-time, and we were out in nature and surrounded by the sea. After years of having your senses abraded by the concrete, nature was so soothing.

First day I arrived was a free day, and I got to swim in the sea. *Swim in the sea* after five years of washing out of the sink once a week. Then I was picking stems off thousands of strawberries and ate so many I shit like a goose, but they were well worth it!

I was assigned to work in the conserve factory, an old barn-like structure fitted out to process the many varieties of fruits and vegetables grown here and also brought across from the mainland because convict labor made it profitable. I did monkey-work, putting lids on cans on a conveyor belt.

Then I volunteered for harder work and hauled fifty-kilo sacks of beans up from the harbor along the cobblestone road to the factory. This work strengthened my muscles and gave me ample opportunity to evaluate the little wooden boats that had brought the beans

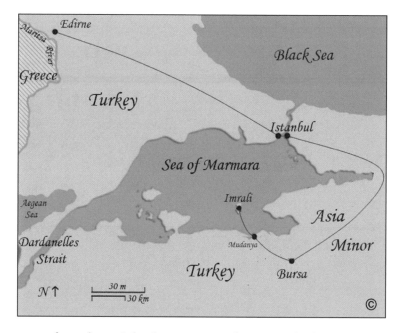

across from the mainland, seventeen miles away. The boats were all hard-working crafts of various sizes and colors, but I noticed each had a little wooden dinghy tied to a rope drifting behind it. The boats weren't allowed to spend the night in the harbor, this being a prison island. But one rainy day after work I was sitting atop a hundred-foot cliff above the village, watching the sea pound against the stone pier below, when I realized the harbor had filled with boats. And more were on their way in. The storm made it too rough for them out at sea, and the prison authorities allowed this exception to the rule. So the boats, with their little dinghies bobbing along behind them, would be spending the night.

Weeks passed as I continued to work in the factory, haul sacks of beans up from the ships, and watch the sky for a storm. My plan was to hide in a tomato processing area near the harbor. Five large concrete bins were used to store the paste, and I knew the one on the end was empty. I could hide inside and watch the harbor while avoiding the patrolling guards.

One cloudy September evening after work, while the other men went to dinner, I raced back to the barracks and changed into my blue jeans and the sneakers I'd inked black for my disastrous window escape attempt with Harvey Bell. I folded my tattered map of Turkey in some wax paper and slipped it into my handmade leather carrying pouch, along with my address book and wallet. I strapped the pouch tightly to my side and pulled on a dark turtleneck sweater.

Checking to be sure I was alone, I reached beneath my mattress and pulled out the short pointed paring knife I'd stolen from the factory. I wrapped paper around the blade and shoved it into the pocket of my jeans. Then I strolled out along one of the trails, just another prisoner enjoying nature before the evening curfew. The night count was a lot less rigid than the morning count. There were a variety of reasons prisoners might be out beyond the night count.

When my path took me near the tomato paste bins, I stopped and stretched and looked around. I glanced into the bin. Then I jumped inside.

It was cool and slick and dark. I huddled on the bottom as the sky turned black above me. At times I poked my head above the rim and checked the harbor. I knew there were no boats coming in tonight, but my trial run seemed to be working out well.

Then I heard footsteps, the measured tread of a guard on the rocky beach. I squatted motionless, not breathing. If he looked inside, what could I say? I felt the maps, the knife. I prayed he wouldn't stop. He passed by.

When the sound of his footsteps faded, I jumped out of the bin and dashed back to the barracks before the curfew. I wasn't disappointed with the evening. It seemed like a solid plan. All I needed now was a storm.

Then on October 2, 1975, four months after arriving on Imrali, I woke to the sound of wind and rain beating against the windowpanes of my barracks. I looked out at the gray sky and my heart began to pound. This was the day!

I worked in the factory, stacking cases, until lunch, then raced back down to the harbor. Rain beat against my face. The storm was worsening, and the half-dozen boats we'd unloaded earlier had already dropped anchor and snugged up, and more were heading in. If only the storm would keep up until after dark.

The storm swirled around me at 5:30 when the guards released us from work, and I cat-footed my way down the wet cobblestones to the harbor. The sea was rough and choppy with anchored boats strung out all over, little dinghies bobbing wildly behind each of them.

Around 9:00 that night, curfew time, I had on my old jeans, black sneakers, and dark turtleneck sweater and was near the harbor in a squat stone building where the night shift did the accounting work. Just a couple of nerdy guys with adding machines while some big-time *kapidyes*, gangster prisoners who virtually ran the prison, hung out until the wee hours of the morning, talking, smoking and drinking.

"*Ich,*" said Big Mustafa, handing me a joint the size of a snow cone. I'd long ago learned how much power and freedom these big-time gangsters had in the Turkish prison system and had made friends with Mustafa the first week. As the only foreigner on the island, and with my amusingly bad but conversationally good Turkish, I was a novelty there.

"No, thanks," I said, "I'm still on my sportsman regime." I'd told everyone I was only here on Imrali for a short time, until America transferred me back home, and that I was getting healthy for my return. This sounded logical enough since there was a Prisoner Exchange Treaty being negotiated between the two countries at the time, and the Turkish prisoners never quite believed I'd gotten thirty years for smuggling only two kilos of hash, anyway. Yeah, welcome to the club. But it also took suspicion off my real reason for being there, because I wasn't waiting for any damn treaty to get signed. I was done with waiting. Mustafa had made arrangements with the guards, and although I didn't much enjoy the smoky card games and partying done in the accounting shed, it gave me a valid reason for being out of my cellblock after lockdown.

I passed the joint to cross-eyed Emir, who was hunched over an adding machine, calculating the profits from that day's canning operation.

"Besides," I told Mustafa, "I don't feel very good. My stomach is weird."

"It's all that exercise you do," said Mustafa, knocking back a small shot of Raki and patting his ample paunch. "Got to relax more."

I doubled over, shoved a finger down my throat and gagged— "Uuurrraagghhhh!"

Mustafa leaped back, moving well for a big man, so his shiny black shoes wouldn't get splattered.

"Think I'll find Charise and go to bed," I said, straightening, wiping my mouth and heading for the door.

Charise was the raggedy old night guard who acted like a servant to these *kapidyes*. He was supposed to keep us locked in the accounting shed until we finished, then escort us back to the cellblocks, but the accounting shed was never locked because the *kapidyes* liked to take little strolls in the night air.

But not this night. The rain beat down in sheets as I opened the door and quickly stepped outside.

"Tell me if you need anything," I heard Mustafa say, as the door closed and the wind swirled around me. There was no sign of Charise. I figured him to be in a small storage shed to the north. I headed south over the wet cobblestones and scurried down to the harbor.

Rain beat against the gray concrete wall of the tomato paste bin. I looked out towards the churning, wind-lashed water, then saw the spotlight swinging toward me. I slipped over the wall of the concrete bin, dropped down and crouched in a corner. The passing spotlight swept over me and threw crazy shadows on the wall. I'd wait until well after curfew to be sure other prisoners wouldn't be around. I figured I had until morning count before anyone noticed me missing. I'd just swim out to the farthest boat, untie its dinghy and then row for the Asian shore.

Yeah, right...

Time crawled by. I had to piss, so aimed it across into the far corner. The urine mingled with the rain puddles, then trickled back across the floor of the bin and settled around my feet. I really didn't care.

I peeked over the top of the bin. The searchlight at the end of the pier sliced through the stormy night and dragged along the rocky shoreline. I waited till it passed, then slowly raised one leg over the edge of the bin.

A noise! I froze when I heard the sharp, staggered clattering of stones—a soldier patrolling the rocky beach. I dropped down into the bin. The sound got closer and closer, then I heard the guard step in under the wooden overhang and shuffle over beside my hiding place. I stopped breathing. A bright orange glow flared up, flickered in the wind and went out. The guard coughed, I could smell the smoke. He was right on the other side of the wall. I tried not to send out any human vibrations. I'm a stone, an inanimate object. Then he finished his butt and moved away. My heart was racing.

The rain got heavier. It soaked me to the skin. The wind was icy. I huddled at the bottom of the bin and screwed up my courage. I started to rise, then thought I heard another noise. I froze again, listening above the howling wind. It must have been my imagination. Time to bite the bullet. If you're going, you're going. I slipped out of the bin and slithered down the bank toward the water, crawling on my belly over a mixture of broken stones, rotting tomato pulp and muddy, puddled earth. I was covered with slime but in the open, exposed to the searchlight, and each time it passed over I dug into the muck, pulled my lucky hat over my head and lay motionless.

I finally reached the sea. So much for the easy part. I'd been a surfer and lifeguard in another lifetime, so I wasn't worried about the swim. I was worried about the first fifty yards of it that lay in front of the guard tower. I could see one soldier operating the searchlight while another paced quietly with a machine gun. I was most thankful for the noise of the wind and waves.

I slipped into the cold sea and pushed off from the shore, my heart pounding with the knowledge that there was no going back now. I struggled through the choppy water, afraid to splash and weighed down by my heavy clothes. A wave caught me in the face. I fought back a cough and swam on as the searchlight sliced across the harbor. I stopped, treading water, gulping air, checking my position—behind me the dim lights of the prison; ahead, faintly bobbing lanterns.

I swam on. High curved hulls of large wooden boats loomed up in the darkness, and the small wooden dinghies tethered behind them bounced about wildly in the choppy sea. I pulled myself into a dinghy and collapsed on the bottom, gasping for breath, shivering, while the wind howled and the dinghy rocked in the darkness.

The dinghy strained against the tether that attached it to the boat. My fingers were so cold I could barely hold the paring knife as I reached up to cut the wet sinewy rope. I was kneeling on the rail, bearing down on the rope, when I froze at the sound of a window crashing open above my head. My heart stopped as a Turkish fisherman gargled poisons out of his throat and spit across me into the water.

If he looked down I was dead.

The window creaked on its hinges and banged shut. I sawed frantically at the rope but it wouldn't cut, and I was ready to gnaw the fucker with my teeth when it snapped and the dinghy swirled away.

I pulled a thick wooden oar from below, then realized there weren't any oarlocks—just wooden pegs on the boat and twisted pretzels of rope around the oars.

"Oh, shit!" How does this work?

Easy if I was in Central Park, but the boat was drifting back toward the rocky shore and the guards with the guns. I fumbled around and finally jammed the oars into position. I pulled. An oar missed, the boat lurched. I struggled for balance. I fought down the rising wave of panic, focused myself, braced my feet on the bottom, tried again. The oars caught and the dinghy slowed, then began to move against the drifting current.

Rain lashed down in sheets as I found a rhythm, the little dinghy cutting through the water. I had to steer a careful course down the inside of the horseshoe-shaped island between the huge rocks in the break line and the other fishing boats anchored further south.

My muscles were hardened from years of yoga and from hefting sacks of beans. I focused down onto pulling the oars, keeping the rhythm. I rowed with a fierce determination, and when I looked up I was past the last of the boats, and the edge of the island had slid by and the prison lights were pinpoints in the darkness. I was out of the harbor into the open sea, beyond the bounds—*Free!* for the first time in five years.

A surge of joy and pent-up emotion burst out of me. Water instantly leapt up into the little boat. I laughed at the irony of drowning now that I was finally free. I leaned into the oars and rowed away from the lights of the island into the dark, swirling night.

I was lost in the stormy darkness, struggling across heavy swells that rolled in like watery monsters out of the night. The wind whistled and threw salt spray into my face. I found myself chanting aloud as I rowed:

If they catch me, they'll beat me,
shoot me,
If I make it, I'm free
free, free...

I stopped rowing, exhausted, and the current nearly ripped an oar from my hand. I dragged the oars into the dinghy, but the fingers of my right hand didn't work, and I had to pry them off the oar. I'd been pulling harder with the right, knowing I had to battle the current that flowed down from the North, forcing me away from the coast. I tied a handkerchief around the bloody right palm then leaned back and drank the rain.

The dinghy took a long swooping drop then rose sideways up the face of a huge rolling swell. I grabbed the seat, terrified, as we hung suspended for a moment, then plunged down the other side. Another long swell lifted beneath me like a rising whale. From the top of the beast I saw, faintly in the far distance, red pinpoints of light. I looked gratefully to The Sky, grabbed the oars and plunged down the backside of the wave.

I rowed. I rowed with fixed determination. All that mattered was to keep pulling, keep going, keep the rhythm. Hours passed. My body stopped complaining. I was beyond pain. I literally had my life back in my own hands, and I exalted in the movement!

Suddenly, the storm was breaking up and a glorious sun was rising. The oar hit something, and the dinghy scraped up on a sandy beach. I dragged it above the tide line and dropped down to hug its salty bow. I loved this little boat and hoped it would get back to its owner.

I rested there a moment, looking at the wild rugged coastline, the surrounding hills, the gulls wheeling in the blue sky above the dark sea. But in the hazy distance I could see Imrali Island, and the rising sun reminded me that the search would soon be on. I got up and sucked salt air deep into my lungs. I set off trotting towards the sun. Ahead of me stretched the deserted north coast of Asia Minor. This was the finest morning of my life.

7

Scrambling Back to Istanbul

On and on I ran, the shore still wild and deserted, my face and arms caked with sweat. I found a small pool of water on some rocks against the cliff. I tested a handful—fresh!—then buried my face and slaked my burning thirst.

Dancing between huge boulders and breaking waves, I worked my way around a headland that jutted out into the sea. I rounded the point, looked up, and was stopped in my tracks by the sight in the hills before me of a Turkish military base! I stared at the tall radio antennae with their blinking red lights—my markers in the night. I smiled in spite of the fear, but the smile quickly faded when I realized I'd have to scale the headland to circle the base.

I was 200 feet above the beach, climbing, clinging to small brush while loose stones and mud skittered beneath my old sneakers. It seemed insane, but I kept finding a smile on my face. There was sunlight above me as I worked my way up a narrow angled ravine near the top. I glanced back down at the beach and sea sparkling below. I lifted myself onto a stone shelf where a wet glistening spider web draped across my face.

I screamed and slipped off the shelf, sliding backwards for several terrifying feet before my hand clutched a gnarled root. I stopped rigid, hung there a beat, then slowly dragged myself back up onto the shelf.

At the top of the ravine I headed into the forested hills that lay beyond the military base. When the sun was high overhead, I emerged from the trees onto tilled fields, where I could see peasants working in the distance, farmers herding sheep. Ahead, around a bend of dirt road, was a small village.

Where the dirt road became cobblestone, an old man puffing on a long curved pipe was crouched down against a white plastered wall. I approached slowly, nervously glancing around.

"Good morning, Father," I said in Turkish. "How can I get to Istanbul?"

The old man eyed me. "Where'd you learn Turkish?"

I did a quick evaluation. "Sagmalcilar prison."

He grinned, then asked knowingly, "For hashish?"

I nodded.

His grin turned to a frown. "You want to buy hashish?"

"No, Baba," I laughed, "I'm not interested in any hash. I just need a ride to Istanbul."

He smiled and pointed to a battered, yellow VW van where farmers were loading sacks of onions and produce on the roof.

"They're going to market at Mudanya. You can catch a bus from there."

The inside of the van was packed with peasants. I asked the driver, "Bursa?"

"Six lira," he replied.

I paid, squeezed into the back seat against the window, the door slammed shut, and the van lurched forward.

The van bounced along the twisting, mountainous road that led up towards Bursa. Everyone was talking and laughing and gesturing with their hands, particularly the driver, who would often turn in his seat to make his point.

On the outside turns the van would sway dangerously towards the edge of the cliffs. It seemed I was looking straight down. How ridiculous, I thought again, to die in a car crash now that I'm finally free. But the driver knew his road, and all I could do was hang on for the ride.

A bottle of scented water was passed around, each filthy farmer vigorously splashing some on his face and neck. Like that helped. I accepted the bottle and did the same, then sat staring out the dirty cracked window, feeling a strange mixture of fear and joy.

Finally Bursa came into view. Its streets were hot and drying, lined with crumbling buildings in the old Turkish style and an occasional Western-style office building that was also falling apart.

A battered cab sat at the curb. I approached carefully.

"Istanbul?"

"Seven hundred fifty lira."

"Four hundred fifty." It was all I had.

"*Yok.* Seven hundred."

I shrugged. The cabbie pointed to the bus station. "Twenty-five lira," he said.

Right, but they'd be looking for me at the bus station.

I had no choice. I had to get to Istanbul. Sure enough, as I approached the bus station I could see two policemen standing out front.

I walked past them. They seemed to ignore me. Lucky for me, information traveled slowly in Turkey in those days.

I bought a ticket. Thirty minutes until the bus left. I found a snack counter and bought a chocolate bar and a big bag of pretzels. I was starving.

We finally boarded the bus which seemed to sit there forever while it filled with chattering passengers. I breathed easier when we left the station and headed for the open road that swung around the eastern edge of the Sea of Marmara on its way to Istanbul.

The late afternoon sun glinted off minaret towers as the Istanbul skyline came into view. We crossed the dark, rushing waters of the Bosphorus on the long, high-arcing span of the Yeni Kopru Bridge joining Asia to Europe, and once again I was back where it had all started five years before. I stepped from the bus and wandered the noisy crowded streets, amazed at the sights, the sounds, the smells; tossed between euphoria and paranoia. I made my way to a seedy hotel where my old prison friend, Johann, was working as manager. Johann had become a Muslim, spoke great Turkish and owed me big time for saving him from a bad beating in prison. I knew he would hide me until things quieted down.

I walked into the lobby. Behind the desk a baldheaded Turk looked up.

"Johann?" I asked. "I'm looking for Johann."

He eyed my clothes. "Johann, you just missed him, he left yesterday for Afghanistan."

Numb, tired and dazed, I stumbled out into the street. What the fuck was I going to do now? This was as far as my plan went. I wanted to collapse, to just find a corner and cry, but that was not an option at the moment.

I noticed several people staring at my blonde hair and moustache. I entered a drugstore and bought a tube of cheap black hair dye, then found a shabby hotel down near the water.

A pockmarked desk clerk looked up as I entered.

"God is great," I said, in Turkish.

The clerk checked me out then gave the ritual response, "God is great. You want a room?"

"Yes, a room. A cheap one."

"The only kind we have," said the clerk, exposing brown, stained teeth. "Luggage?"

I hesitated. "I lost it."

"Passport?"

"It was in my luggage."

He stared at me. "One hundred lira," he said, dropping a key on the counter.

It was robbery, but I paid.

Upstairs in my dingy little room I found a smile flickering across my face as I turned the key in the lock. It looked like a palace to me. I wedged a chair against the door and checked out the drop to the alley below the window. Then I stood in front of the bathroom mirror with cotton balls in one hand and the black dye in the other, struggling through the instructions written in Turkish. Something about applying the paste to the inside of your wrist and waiting twenty-four hours for any allergic reaction.

I didn't really have time for that.

I poured the inky liquid that smelled like cat piss onto the cotton, then reached up towards my blonde hair.

8

The Scent of Freedom

At dawn the next morning I was on another bus rumbling west out of Istanbul. I sat in the back seat, a newspaper in front of my face, reading by the light of the sun pouring in over my shoulder. When I lowered the paper, anyone looking at me would see gonky black hair framing my gaunt, haggard face. I fit right in with the rest of the group.

The noon sun dropped on a crumpled, water-stained map open on my lap.

I placed my finger on Edirne—an ancient border town a few hundred kilometers east on the Maritsa River separating Turkey and Greece. I traced the river south of Edirne and stopped at a blank space on the map.

I must have dozed off. I woke suddenly as the bus pulled up to a quick halt. A Turkish policeman stepped on and glanced down the aisle. My heart stopped. I sat frozen in my seat, my hand poised on the emergency door.

The policeman scanned the passengers then turned to the driver for his papers and permits. Just a routine check. Everything seemed to be in order. The policeman tipped his hat and left. As the bus started up, my heart began beating again, and I breathed out a sigh of relief.

Edirne was crowded and dirty, with successive layers of culture built on top of each other. The main square was bustling with people when we arrived in the late afternoon, and I noticed many soldiers and policeman mixed in with the crowd.

Across the street from a taxi stand, still behind a newspaper, I scanned the drivers. I approached a young skinny kid with long hair leaning against a maroon '53 Buick.

"Excuse me," I said, in Turkish, "I lost my friends and need a ride south."

The Kid eyed me. "Where'd you learn Turkish?"

"In prison."

"For hashish?" he smiled.

I nodded, glancing around nervously.

"You want some?" asked the Kid, slyly.

"You gotta be kidding," I said in English. Then in Turkish, "No, I just want to join my friends. We're in a campground south of here, beyond a small village called..?"

"Black Kasim?" offered the Kid.

"Right, Black Kasim," I said, anxious to get in the cab. My eyes flickered over to two passing soldiers. The Kid noticed.

"A hundred lira," he said.

"A hundred?"

The Kid just smiled. "The road is very bad."

About ten miles south of Edirne we came to Black Kasim, the last little village on my map, then to a great expanse of wild open borderland on both sides of the river.

The Kid slowed down when he saw some people by the side of the road.

"Where's the campground?" he asked.

They just looked at him in bewilderment. "The campground?"

They shrugged again, and I noticed one of them holding a newspaper with a front-page headline about Imrali. This was a little too close...

"Let's just drive," I told the Kid.

"Wait," he said, "these guys will know."

He pulled in front of a small tavern and yelled up to some men sitting on the porch. "Anybody know where the tourist campground is?"

Amerika'lı William Hayes,
esrar kaçakçılığından
30 yıla mahkum olmuştu

İmralı adasından büyük firar

●Amerika'lı mahkum bir kum motorunun
sandalına saklandı ve açık denizde
teknenin ipini kesti. Yüzerek Yunan adalarına
çıkan Amerika'lı buradan ülkesine döndü

To my horror, three policemen came sauntering down towards the cab. Their collars were open. They had bottles of beer in their hands. One of them leaned a beefy forearm on my window and exhaled a wave of beer breath across me.

"What?" belched Beerbreath.

"Campground, tourist campground?" said the Kid.

I sat very still.

The policeman pulled his head out of the window and looked down the road. He took a sip of beer and looked in the other direction. "No fucking campground here. It's a military zone."

I turned towards the Kid and said, firmly, "Let's just go."

The Kid caught on. "Thanks, Officer, my mistake, I think I know what we want."

I looked back and Beerbreath was staring at us as we pulled away.

At the southern edge of town even the dirt road disappeared.

"I can't go any farther," said the Kid.

"I think my friends are just ahead," I said.

"It'll wreck my car."

"Just a little farther, I'll pay you extra."

The Kid muttered under his breath but jammed the cab into low gear, and we followed the rutted tracks into the low hills.

At sunset we stopped by the edge of a dry cornfield, and I stood on the hood of the old Buick, staring at the hills in the distance. Greece. It had to be Greece. So close I could smell it!

I jumped down from the hood and gave the puzzled Kid several hundred lira, the last of my money. "Thank you, Brother," I said. "I know my friends are camped in those hills."

He looked at the emptiness of the surrounding countryside, shrugged, and pocketed the money.

"May Allah keep you," I said, smiling at him and closing the door.

"Wait!" said the Kid, nodding to the hills. "This isn't a healthy place for you alone at night."

"I'm sure I'll find my friends."

"Then, may Allah keep you," he said, and pulled away, dragging a long plume of dust behind him.

In the fields stretching far off to my right, I could see sheep and a couple of shepherds making their way back towards the village. The bells of the sheep clunked a soft, lazy rhythm that traveled far in the clear autumn twilight. I would have to be very quiet. I stepped into the corn and waited for the coming of night.

9

A River in the Darkness

oving through the darkness over rocky, eroded ground, it was difficult to be quiet or make much progress. I leaned against a tree trunk, exhausted, and peered out at the night. Occasional flashlights blinked in the distance—Turkish soldiers patrolling this tense border. A dog barked somewhere. Dogs? Oh shit, not dogs! I thought it might be quieter if I went barefoot, so I peeled off my tattered sneakers and socks and buried them in a shallow hole at the base of the tree.

"Sniff those," I said, figuring my stinky sneakers would blow out the dogs' noses.

It shows how goofy I was getting, because now I was walking barefoot and my feet were getting chewed up, but freedom was so close now, so near and yet... I found myself moving slowly up a rocky, crumbling slope in a sideways crawl, drenched in sweat, shivering, trying for silence. I came to a drainage ditch just beneath the crest of the hill and slipped down the side of the ditch into deep, soothing mud on the bottom. It felt so good to be off the exposed hill. I snuggled down into the mud to rest, and shortly the air around me was filled with the happy chirping of frogs. I started to pull my way up out of the ditch when I heard—singing! I dropped down into the mud and once again tried to become inanimate, a stone upon the ground not sending out any human vibrations.

Footsteps were moving closer. Two Turkish border guards slowly strolled along the ditch above me, exchanging verses of some folk ditty. My heart was pounding in my ears. I could have reached up and grabbed their ankles.

When the voices faded I lifted out of the ditch and crested the hill in a low crouch. I flitted from clumps of scraggly bushes to small erosion gullies. The air was still. I thought I heard more voices off to the left, so I headed right, into a clump of trees. Through the darkness of the trees I caught a glimmer of light reflecting off metal. I moved closer and quietly parted some branches. Jeeesus Christ! There was a huge hulking tank, crouched like some hungry, waiting animal. Then I saw more tanks beneath camouflage nets. I softly let the branches close and padded off to the left. Let sleeping tanks lie...

Above me a tiny silver sliver of moon flickered through the black canopy of trees as I struggled below in the clutching darkness, lost in a world of tangled undergrowth and cold, slurping mud. I muffled the sound of my labored breathing and moved with cautious desperation, trying for silence. I was cold and tired and terrified of capture, but the thought of freedom drove me on. Nothing short of death would stop me now, and death hardly scared me at all.

A veil of mosquitoes settled on my sweaty face when I stopped in a shallow pool of moonlight. I ignored them, listening...sensing. Somewhere beneath the night hum of insects and frogs I heard the faint burbling sound of running water—the Maritsa. My eyes strained to pierce the gloom. This river in the darkness promised both an end and a beginning for me. It flowed down from the cobalt mountains of Bulgaria and emptied into the blue Aegean sea. Somewhere on the other side was freedom.

I listened for another moment, glancing at the moon to judge direction, then slid back into the undergrowth. Branches gouged my face and brambles cut my bare feet, but I hardly noticed. I'd been awake now for days, but my mind was burning, my senses taut with intensity.

Voices suddenly seared the night. I froze. Soldiers again. They were a distance away but sounded closer than before. I fought to control the irrational fear that screamed for me to run. The soldiers were patrolling but weren't yet aware of me; if I ran, they'd hear me.

My mind knew this, but my body kept quivering, pumping adrenalin, sending out fear vibrations as lethal as blood in the Pacific.

To master my fear I attempted to use it, flowing through it to the image of a sleek cat who moved with my body, stealthy and silent in the night. It worked. The cat glided forward and the voices faded as…time…seemed…to…slow…and existence was measured by the distance to the next branch, by the quiet lifting and placing of a naked foot in the muddy earth. Then wet bushes parted and the black flowing waters of the Maritsa were rushing past in front of me.

I sat on the dank, mossy bank in the thick darkness, picking thorns from my feet, calming my breathing and gathering myself together. It was the night of October 4, 1975, and a black, velvet sky strewn with blue diamond stars stretched high over my head. Frogs chirruped. A loon hooted far out over the water. My old jeans were torn and caked with mud, my sweater was in tatters. I thought about drowning or being shot, and was truly terrified of capture; but again I found myself smiling at the sheer absurdity of the situation, at the Cosmic Joke. Just the realization of being on this frontier riverbank in such a bizarre position made everything all right. I'd always found life interesting, because you never really know what the next moment will bring. That's the reason I rejected suicide as a way out of prison; even at its worst, life is too precious and fragile and tantalizingly unpredictable to throw away. Squatting there like some hunted animal I felt so terribly alive, I thought I'd burst out of my body.

Instead, I took a last deep, deliberate breath, made a deal with The Sky like I always do when in trouble ("Sweet Jesus, I'll be your friend!"), then slipped quietly into the cold, swirling water.

The muddy bottom sucked at my feet, and the rushing water almost knocked me off balance. The cold was numbing but I moved slowly, concentrating, trying for silence. There could be soldiers on either side, and the nationality of the bullet didn't matter.

The water swirled up to my waist, then suddenly got lower. The bottom rose up to another bank. I was in Greece…or was I?

I moved slowly through some trees and came to more water— the real river. It stretched out for several hundred yards, rippling darkly under the starlight. I was just on a little island, not in Greece yet.

But I was close and waded right in. The river was deeper and the current was much stronger. I lashed into it with a fierce breaststroke. The current swept me downstream but I fought against it, angling across the river.

My exhaustion fell away. I thrust my arms and kicked my legs, survival energy surging through me. I couldn't see much in the darkness, and it was hard to judge if I was making any progress. I let the river take me, while angling steadily across its insistent current. I kept kicking until my knee suddenly struck a rock. My feet found bottom. I stood up, bracing myself against the pull of the water. I waded to the sloping riverbank and threw myself down on the freezing mud. I was shivering and terribly afraid, but ecstatic to have crossed that river. A burst of giddy laughter popped out of me and I clamped my hand over my mouth. I climbed the embankment and disappeared into the trees.

I was sleepwalking now. Hungry, tired, cold, wet and confused. I had to move west, but the woods grew thick and thorns dug into my feet. Then the woods became overgrown fields. I heard sounds, voices, I wasn't sure what. I knew the river had shifted and the border changed over the years, and I didn't want to make the mistake of approaching the first person I saw and having him be a Turkish soldier.

Behind me, the eastern sky glowed with faint signs of sunrise. I stumbled onto a dirt road. It felt so soothing to my bruised feet. Dimly, I could see a farmhouse, silhouetted black against the blackness of the trees beyond it. Barking dogs suddenly rushed out at me. I hurried down the road until the dogs stopped following.

I had to get off the road, but the smooth dirt felt so good. Just a little farther and I'd move back into open country. A little farther.

My head throbbed. My body was operating on automatic pilot. I shivered and coughed but kept my feet shuffling along the road. Ahead of me a line of murky trees crowded both sides of the road. I'd stay on the road to the trees, then strike off into the woods again. I padded into the tunnel of trees and didn't see the wooden kiosk until stumbling past it. A bayonet whizzed down in front of my face and quivered there as a sharp voice growled, "Huuhhh!"

Captured! I froze, arms in the air. A startled border guard shouted something I didn't understand. He shouted again, and I realized I didn't understand what he was saying. So he must be speaking Greek. So this must be Greece. So I must be free! I'd made it! I collapsed on the ground with my arms still in the air, grinning like a loon. He jumped back and began blowing a whistle.

Noise, running feet, a circle of flashlights around me. Someone pointing to a watch with a .45 pistol—"Four and a half, man, four and a half. What you doing here?"

"I'm an American. I just escaped from Turkey. I made it! I made it!"

The Greeks held me in an eight by eight-foot cell in the woods for the two weeks it took them to decide my fate. After all, I'd entered the country illegally at 4:30 a.m., covered in mud, without papers, without shoes, and with a bizarre story to explain my presence in their restricted border area.

A leathery old military intelligence officer with piercing hawk eyes came to question me that first morning. I detected a definite attitude in his voice and decided I'd been pushed around enough these past five years—that it was time to assert myself.

"O.K. That's it. No more questions. I know my rights. I'm an American citizen. I demand to see the American Consul. I demand a lawyer. I know my rights."

He smiled a crooked little grin beneath his thick black moustache and blew out a stream of smoke. "Let me tell you what your rights are, *Kid*. We find you in the middle of the night coming out of a totally restricted military zone. You have no papers, no shoes or socks, and you're covered with mud. We could sentence you for entering this country illegally. We could throw you back across the river to the Turks. We could take you out in woods and shoot you. Nobody would ever know. Or, you can shut up and cooperate, and we'll send you home."

"Wellll, when you put it that way," I said with a smile, "...what was it you wanted to know?"

Each day the intelligence officer spent long hours questioning me about Sagmalcilar and Imrali. What about the soldier bases? The color of the soldiers' uniforms? Radar on top of Imrali island? The tanks at the border? I mean, how important could this shit be if *I* knew about it? He pulled out a huge detailed map of the border—it must've had fucking anthills on it. I showed him where I made the crossing.

"You're a very lucky man, William."

"Yeah, I know."

"No, you don't. This entire area here is mined. You could easily have been blown up."

God looks out for saints and fools.

The Greeks could have sentenced me to prison or returned me to Turkey. They graciously deported me instead. There's little love lost between the Greeks and the Turks. I was actually deported for being "a bad influence upon the youth of Greece," the same charge made against Socrates. At least I wasn't asked to drink any hemlock.

10

Harvey and the Warriors of Islam

I had been on Imrali Island for two months when Harvey finally made it back to Sagmalcilar. Harvey knew Sagmalcilar hadn't been lucky for him, but at least he'd have access to the American Consul and better medical care in Istanbul than out in the wilds of Antakya. And getting better medical care had given Harvey an idea—a new plan for escape. The problem was surviving until he could test the plan.

His old nemesis, Arief the Bonebreaker, had been waiting in the transport room the hot August afternoon Harvey arrived back from Antakya. When Harvey stepped from the back of the baking metal van—dirty, unshaven, and covered with sweat—the dark, burning eyes in Arief's hatchet face seared into him.

Harvey coughed and stumbled as the soldiers pulled his chains and led him to check-in. Arief stood silently as a burly guard named Ahmet patted Harvey down, searching for contraband or weapons.

"Should I strip him?" asked Ahmet.

Harvey turned to Arief and automatically began opening his pants, then he was wracked by a fit of coughing. Arief turned away, disgusted.

"Take this trash away."

Harvey just stood there, his pants still open, staring into space—looking like a sick, broken man.

But the Sagmalcilar authorities hadn't forgotten the circumstances around Harvey's last stay, so they decided to keep him in a

Hi Willie

    I reopened this letter because after I had written it I realized I had exagerated and read some dreams into the seams. Yah, six months living in an isolated cellblock w/ 2 arab terrorists was, as I look back, the wierdest time I've spent in prison. Briefly (cause I've only got one sheet of paper) it came to an enormous conclusion when the PLO pulled its bloody bus ride in Israel.

    You may recall I came here because (right! I'm still here. They're gone) (?) it seemed a quiet place to practice my guitar and I figured I could co-exist with anyone after 4 yrs with the Turks. Then I got "caught up", or facinated by, their celebrity and all the terrorist goings on and Carlos and Wadi Hadad and the stories (and my mind cried § There's a story in these guys) (and there is, I'm sure). But then they and I got down to nitty political discussions and beneath their marxist gloss I discovered a primer coat of village backwardness and arab nationalism slapdashed over a general ignorance of history and political reality. They thought Stalin was a right guy and if he fucked over a few million people then it was for the good of world communism; yet they could never convince me he was anything but a fascist and that Russia and China were in actuality no more than dictatorships. Naturally, I've never been able to change an Arab's mind about anything so I became, in their eyes, a fascist and they seemed more and more to me to be incapable of logical reasoning. ultra brief. Two european communists, a Swiss small isolated wing with Borhan and Metti, two young Arab terrorists, "warriors of Islam," who'd attacked the Istanbul airport a few months earlier. Harvey had seen their pictures in the papers while he was at Antakya. These guys were big-time celebrities in the prison—vibrant Muslim crusaders, black-belt karate experts and soldiers of God. Harvey thought it was all a load of shit.

"You blew up innocent people," he said to Borhan, in Turkish, the first night they sat down for dinner.

Borhan, built like a bull, tore a chunk of bread from the loaf and dipped it into his thick lentil soup. "Blood of the innocents will wash the stain from the nation of Islam."

Harvey stared at him. "You fucking asshole," he said, pleasantly, in English.

Borhan looked up from his plate. "Fookinazgol?"

Borhan turned to Metti, a wiry, intense fellow who had barely acknowledged Harvey since his arrival.

"Fuck-ing ass-hole, means.." said Metti, in English, staring at Harvey, then switching to Arabic... "*Kasorgtak, Sharmuta!*"

Borhan stood abruptly and swept his plate from the table. Harvey listened to the metal plate rattling on the stone floor as Borhan stood quivering with rage in front of him.

Guess these guys don't get called asshole that often, thought Harvey. He remembered about first impressions and his escape plan and began coughing and hacking, a sick, broken man getting worse.

Metti put a hand on Borhan's arm. He said something in Arabic and they both laughed. Borhan pulled Harvey's soup across the table and tore off another hunk of bread. Harvey coughed his way out of the room and almost kicked himself for forgetting his game plan and the cover he needed to establish. The sooner he got away from these two loonies, the better.

And then one October morning the little metal window in the gray iron door slid open and Harvey heard Osman, a lowly guard he'd befriended, calling his name. Osman and Harvey had done some business on the side, but this was too obvious to be a business deal.

"God is great," said Harvey, approaching the door.

"God is great," said Osman, passing rolled-up newspapers in through the window. "Big news."

Harvey passed Osman the customary pack of cigarettes and opened the copy of *Hürriyet*. The entire front page was the story of Billy's "Escape From Imrali Island." There was the mug shot picture of a young Billy and the colored drawing of a bare-chested, muscled, blonde prisoner in a rowboat, slashing a big knife across the tether of a looming fishing boat.

Harvey burst out laughing. "Yeesss!!!" he screamed, leaping in the air, waving the newspaper above his head. A sharp pain in his groin settled him down. He opened the copy of *Günyadin* with yet another story of the escape, including a photo of Billy's actress/girl-friend accomplice "Jane", and his "route" on a map.

"What happened?" he asked Osman through the window. "Does it say what happened after he got off the island?"

"They don't know. I heard they found a rowboat on the beach near Bursa, but there's no news of Billy."

"Who's this girl?"

"Says some actress girlfriend who helped him."

Harvey was torn with conflicting emotions. He was elated for his friend, but worried about his safety. He was thrilled Billy was free, but despondent that he, himself, was still in jail. The air was suddenly too thick to breathe and the walls leaned in on him.

"Thanks, Osman, let me know if you hear any news."

He turned from the window and Osman called out, "*Getchmis olsun.*" ("May it pass quickly.")

Harvey nodded and stumbled out into the small, empty courtyard. A bright yellow slice of morning sunlight ran diagonally across the gray concrete wall at one end of the rectangle. Harvey leaned back against the warming wall and turned up to the sun. Tears slowly slipped out from beneath his closed eyes and trickled down his face.

11

Dream Come True

November, 1975: It was a glorious Indian summer in New York. I was living at my brother Rob's place on the lower east side of Manhattan, sleeping on the couch. I woke and stretched in the pre-dawn darkness, smiling and feeling refreshed. Five-thirty a.m.—three hours sleep. It was enough. I had little need for sleep since escaping from prison a month before. Too many things to do.

The living room was chilled, but when I slipped from beneath the blanket and stood naked on the rug, I wasn't cold. I'd come to terms with The Cold during my first winter Inside. I had a hefty morning erection which I whacked against my leg a few times just for fun before padding quietly into the bathroom.

At the sink I turned on the hot water tap.

It was easy. Just a twist of the wrist.

Amazingly simple, yet simply amazing after five years of cold-water mornings. I watched the steaming water flow for a moment before adding a little cold. I washed my face and snorted some water through each nostril like I'd learned from the yoga books. I squeezed a big hunk of Colgate onto my new blue brush. In the mirror I brushed and took stock of my mouth. The shareholders wouldn't be happy. Five teeth gone in as many years, the rest in desperate need of attention. My vanity was thankful that the front teeth were holding out better than the back molars, so my mouth didn't look as bad as it really was. The problem, of course, is that you can't chew with vanity.

I looked at the face in the mirror. It was thin but not as gaunt as it had been a month before. That fevered intensity about the eyes I wrote off as still being alive. The pale blonde hair on my newly sheared head and even shorter fuzz on my lip were starting to grow. I was beginning to look like me again. I smiled at myself. The mirror smiled back. I brushed my teeth. I brushed the mirror's teeth. I felt silly and wonderfully alive and free.

I spread a towel on the living room rug and stood quietly with eyes closed, listening to my heart. It's a slow heart, only beating about fifty times a minute. I listened until I could hear it steady and clear in my ears, pumping blood to all parts of my body. "Awake!" I whispered to my body from the little control room in my mind. "Rise!" I said and rose onto my toes, watching my hands reach far up above my head. At the top of the stretch I held for a moment, poised, enjoying the muscle play in my legs, butt, back and arms, savoring the simple act of balance. The releasing movement was cat-stretching sensual down onto the towel, each of my vertebrae clicking as I arched my back and pressed my groin to the floor.

Yoga had become my morning ritual and helped me remain healthy and reasonably sane during my prison years. I'd first learned about it in the Sixties from Crazy Carol, a hippie girlfriend at Marquette University. When my ankles had started crackling and I was waking with stiffness in my joints, I knew immediately it must be arthritis, and I was only twenty-one, much too young to be crippled. I figured the arthritis crept down around my bones and joints at night so that stretching and cracking each morning was necessary just to stay even.

I made a tripod of my arms and stood on my head. This changed the flow of blood and stimulated my brain. I breathed easy as images of Amsterdam floated through my mind...

...The lights of Schiphol Airport twinkled in the night as my flight from Thessaloniki, Greece—with a quick frightening change in Frankfurt—descended. When the jet touched down in Amsterdam I had a new passport in one pocket, courtesy of the

American Consul in Thessaloniki, Jim Murray, and a thousand dollars in the other, thanks to my ever-steady father in New York. Jim had brought me some of his own clothes—a warm sweatshirt, some jeans, a pair of old sneakers.

I was slightly nervous as the line of passengers filed toward the Dutch customs counter. I wasn't used to being out among people again and had acquired a certain dislike for customs. A young woman in front of me had burning black hair that smelled like summer lilacs. I wanted to lift the heavy tresses and let them flow through my fingers but resisted the impulse. I glanced down at my passport photo, still shocked by the grim, gaunt face staring up at me.

The young blonde customs agent stamped my passport with barely a glance. I passed through baggage claim empty-handed and merged with the bustling flow of people heading for the buses. My senses were still on prison alert, but the nervousness faded when I sensed no danger. Instead of fear and anger in the air, there were happy bursts of laughter as waiting loved ones greeted new arrivals. The black-haired girl rushed into a young man's arms, and their urgency rippled through my body. I felt like radar, sending out this questing pulse of energy; or like a tuning fork, throbbing with the vibrations of everything around me, bombarded by all the stimuli pouring in—smells, colors, shapes and sounds, dogs, shops, people's faces. I glided along the polished stone floor in Jim's old shoes like a sensation-starved sponge, soaking up the fresh, vibrant life swelling around me. I trembled with excitement, yet felt so serene. I was content just to be part of this moving crowd, a free man boarding a bus and going where he pleased.

The rambling old train station near the docks was bustling when we pulled in, noisy with people, taxis, and clanging tram cars. I stepped off the bus like a child at a fair, already glowing from the simple street scenes that had flashed so wondrously past my window on the ride from the airport. The still night air was crisp on my face and city-sweet to my nose. Sounds carried clearly—voices calling, horns tooting, bicycles jingling on the cobbles. I turned a slow full circle on the sidewalk, saturating my senses. Freedom had been a burning need for five years. Now I was free and needed nothing. It was a glorious feeling. I felt pure, elated.

I'd dreamed of freedom for so long that the outside world had become a dream. Now I was out, and it was like being in my dream come true.

I began walking. Direction didn't matter. Wherever I went, whatever happened next, was fine with me. I followed my feet, flowing with the crowd down winding stone streets that bridged dark, still canals. There was perfume on the breeze and the wafting scents of frying foods. I'd been in Amsterdam years before, but that seemed like another lifetime. I was different now. I felt brand new and was seeing everything for the first time. The soft night glowed with shop lights and streetlamps and the flickering candles of corner cafes. Music drifted in the air. I stared into the faces of approaching people and they all thrilled me. My eyesight was phenomenal. In an instant I drank in every line, curve, and feature of each person passing by. They were total strangers, yet I felt I knew each of them intimately. I wanted to take each face—young, old, man, woman, smooth, wrinkled, happy, sad—hold it in my hands and whisper, "It's all right. We're alive. We're alive here on this street in Amsterdam, and everything is all right."

I found myself in the red light district, wandering through rows of quaint stone houses that had stood side by side above the narrow streets and quiet canals for 300 years. Many of the ground-level rooms now had soft red or blue lights glowing behind curtained bay windows. When the heavy drapes were open, there was a woman in each room. They were all beautiful women, even the ugly ones. They lounged on satin sheets and beckoned with their bodies. Dark nipples stood erect on plump breasts; tight sequined G-strings gleamed between lush silken thighs; pouting red mouths formed around the pressure I felt growing in my pants. I walked the street slowly, staring in the windows, mesmerized by the sight of so much femininity. It wasn't difficult to turn down their gracious offers. I was only looking. It was enough—almost too much. Even before prison I loved to look at prostitutes but never went with them. I had to believe a woman was with me because she wanted to be, not because I'd paid her. I'd savored the idea of being with a woman for five long years, but felt no urgency now. Just standing there on that cobbled street, I was in such a state of bliss that all things seemed equally amazing, and I was content to let them come with their own time.

Still, after five years Inside, the back alleys of Amsterdam were blowing my circuits. One thin black girl on a white fur bed was so stunning I couldn't stop staring at her. She did nothing, she had to do nothing. After a while, when she knew I was a gawker and not a buyer, she moved slowly toward the window, smiled at my silly gaping face, and drew the curtains.

I moved on to the next window.

It was getting late when some funky saxophone music drew me to the dimly lit doorway of a small hotel bar. It was a shabby place, but looked like a mansion to me. A few people sat around talking and drinking beer from wet, glistening steins while Wilson Pickett moaned from the jukebox. The place felt right. The plump blonde barmaid moved with a slow, easy grace. I drank her in as she poured a cold draft. She looked up and smiled.

"I'd like a room for a few nights. And a shower. Please."

The key she took from the pigeonhole in the wall behind her had a battered wooden knob attached to it with a black "15" painted on its side. "Top floor. Shower's across the hall. Twenty guilders a night."

The narrow, winding stairs flashed me back to a small attic room beneath the eaves of an old house in Milwaukee. That had been a magical place, my first time living alone. Tiny Room 15 also felt magical as I opened the door and switched on the overhead light. It was clean and sparse with crisp white sheets on a small bed against a slanting yellow plaster wall. A squat old dresser sat solidly on the dark plank floor; a fading throw rug lay beneath a pot-bellied porcelain sink in a corner; and a full-length wood-framed window occupied most of the wall across from the bed.

I locked the door behind me and dropped my small package of recently purchased toiletries on the sheets. I switched off the light and stood before the open window, gazing out across the treetops and slanting tile roofs of the darkened city. Church bells tolled in the distance, deep-toning the soft night. I felt secure. Alone. Yes, finally, alone. In prison you were always lonely, but never alone. There were always people around you—watching, aware, waiting. It nearly drove me mad.

I stripped off my grimy clothes. Naked and alone in the darkness, I touched myself without guilt or fear for the first time in five years. It felt incredible. My body was muscled and alive, the skin tingling beneath my hands. I switched the light back on and pondered my reflection in the window. I hadn't really seen my body in a long time. I'd stared at my face in a small hand mirror like most guys in prison, searching for some reassurance of identity, but it wasn't healthy to stand around naked gazing at your own reflection.

Now I turned slow circles before the window, loving the sight of myself. It was erotic, but the excitement was more than sexual. I'd always appreciated my body as the channel of sensual pleasure, but now my body was almost like an old friend, one who'd been strong for me, who'd supported me through the bad times and had finally carried me to freedom. My friend and I had worked hard to stay healthy in prison. If you were sick, you were weak; if you were weak, you were prey. But now we were free and dirty, and after five years of washing from a grungy sink with a plastic pitcher, we were about to take a shower...

...When I rolled down from the headstand, my stimulated brain and I lay on the floor of my brother's apartment in New York, staring up at the ceiling. I quickly ran through the words of a prayer I'd devised for myself in prison: "I rise to this day with joy, knowing I'm closer to the God within me, conscious of myself, aware; my being is bound by truth, expressed in action, expanded through experience, strengthened in sorrow, rapt with joy; at one with the All, at peace with the world; my purpose for being is to love." If nothing else, the words provided some inspiration and focus for the coming day. And my focus, as usual, was shifting again. Since escaping, I noticed I couldn't sit still long enough to really meditate, but I figured I'd had enough interior work to last for a while—now there was all that Outside world to taste, touch, lick, smell and feel. The streets of Manhattan called to me, lured me out with endless possibilities.

12

Coming Home

The sun was rising as I wheeled Rob's black 10-speed bicycle onto 14th Street. The air was crisp and still, the city just waking to the day. A garbage truck rumbled and clanked on the corner, enjoying its breakfast piled high on the curb. I skirted a thin column of steam that curled lazily from a Con Ed manhole, then nodded to an old black guy alone at the bus stop. He nodded back as a battered blue *Daily News* truck rattled past me, slowing only slightly to toss a huge wired bundle of papers at a rickety wooden kiosk that seemed to grow out of the sidewalk. I hung a right on 1st Avenue and headed uptown.

The streets began to buzz. The city was stirring—I could feel it right up through the rubber tires, through the frame of the bike. Women were stirring, millions of them— out there in those apartments above me, waking to the day, stretching their long, naked legs.

I hit a pothole and nearly ruptured myself. "Goddamn!" I made a mental note to keep my eyes open on these New York streets.

I pedaled slowly, three pumps then an easy glide. The streets weren't clogged yet with rush hour traffic, so I could watch the city flowing around me without too much risk of being crushed under a bus. I was headed for 59th Street and the bike paths of Central Park. I wasn't hungry, but my taste buds tingled as I rode past delicatessens, supermarkets, pizza places, donut shops, Greek diners, French cafes and umbrellaed hot dog stands. I glowed at the thought of being able to stop anywhere, anytime, and eat whatever I desired.

All my cravings could be satisfied out on the street. I had a flash of waking from a dream in the fetid heat of a summer prison night with the frustrating, tantalizing taste of cold applesauce on my tongue. The 23rd Street light was changing against me, but I put on a burst of speed and flashed through the intersection. Rob's bike was a joy to ride—light, strong and delicate. It gave me mobility. I loved mobility—to move in a straight line more than thirty-four paces without facing up against a gray stone wall was sheer ecstasy.

I turned west on 34th Street, heading toward the Empire State Building. On the corner of 2nd Avenue, a bum in a soiled raincoat and battered black sneakers was foraging in a garbage can. He glanced up as I passed and I got a quick shot of burning dark eyes in a dirty gray beard. Rasputin of the gutters. I guess the city was medium filthy—scraps and bottles everywhere, soiled bits of papers on the breeze, trash hanging out of cans, dog shit in the streets. I soaked it all up and loved it. It was New York filth, New York dog shit—I was home!

I turned right on 5th Avenue and leaned into the pedals. The bike leapt beneath me. It was twenty-five blocks to the park, straight uptown against one-way traffic. Not the easiest route, but it got my blood pumping. The street was filling with buses and trucks and hurtling yellow taxicabs. Speed was essential for me. I could out-maneuver these metal monsters if I kept the momentum. I focused my radar down to immediate matters and sent out a cone of awareness. I couldn't watch faces in the bustling morning crowd or gaze at the buildings gleaming high above me in the blue sky. If I didn't concentrate fully on the street, there was a good chance I'd become part of it.

I strained at the pedals. I was flying...39th Street...40th...the next few blocks were slightly downhill. I flashed past the huge stone lions crouched in front of the New York Public Library. The wind rushed by me. A door opened on an illegally parked car. I barely touched the handlebars. Flick-flick. Just a shift of the wrists and I was around him.

Approaching 42nd Street the light went orange and the crowd leaned toward the street. No problem. A green Volkswagen jumped the signal and pulled into the street in front of me. No problem. I saw the huge pothole too late and instinctively swerved toward the curb to avoid it. Now I had a problem. I was committed to the speed, far beyond any braking point. I was also too far on the right to pass both the crowd and the car on the left, as I'd intended. Instant decision time. A space was about to open between the first three people already in the street and the rest still on the curb. I watched it happening like a broken-field runner in a football game watches the moving pattern. Thank God, again, for high school sports. I picked the hole, aimed the bike and flashed through.

I heard gasps behind me but couldn't even shout an apology. The woman in the green VW had finally seen me hurtling down on her from the blindside and had jammed on her brakes. I swerved past her back bumper on the slippery edge of control, then straightened up and shot toward the trees of Central Park.

Gliding from the concrete streets onto the cool, shaded bike paths of the park was like diving underwater. The smooth black asphalt of Poets' Row was matted with a carpet of yellow-orange leaves. I coasted silently through a tunnel of trees with brilliant foliage above and below. Brown sparrows flickered among the branches, and busy gray squirrels rummaged on the ground. The sounds of the city faded as I drifted further into the park.

A young dreadlocked kid was standing alone on Promenade Bridge. He held up a joint. "Hey, Mon, you want some smoke? Got da 'erb."

I smiled and cruised past him.

"Taste it, Mon, it's Lamb's Bread."

Now he had me. Lamb's Bread? I never heard that term before. I turned the bike in a tight circle and slid up beside him. Two quick hits off the joint. *Boinnggg!* These lambs are some kind of bakers.

He had five big joints in his hand. "You want some? Cheap, Mon."

"No, but thanks for the Lamb's Bread."

He smiled and slowly cupped the bulge in his crotch. "Anyting else I can do for you, den?"

I smiled and pedaled down a side path heading for the lake. I figured I could afford a toke this morning. I didn't plan any work until a noon meeting with Julian Bach, my newly acquired literary agent. He'd been reading the first fifteen pages of a book I was writing about my prison experience. I'd met with a number of literary agents but chose Julian because he reminded me of Mr. Chips—a distinguished, avuncular figure. At the first meeting in his office, I saw a smiling photo of him running around the Reservoir. That settled it for me.

I let the bike glide to a stop next to a peeling wooden bench. Some brown ducks were quacking softly far out on the lake. Nearby, two white swans drifted past, silently trailing their wakes along the smooth surface. A gull flapped calmly across the sky from east to west, and I remembered flying in from Amsterdam two weeks before...

...I was at a window seat as the huge Pan Am jet left the blue Atlantic and crossed low over the eastern tip of Long Island. Montauk Point passed beneath me—the black rocks, the gleaming white lighthouse, the beach I'd surfed in high school. I used to drive to Montauk late Friday nights, after a date, in our Volkswagen with my surfboard strapped to the roof. I'd make my way down the dark, rutted dirt roads to the cliffs above the sea and curl up asleep in a blanket on the back seat with the ocean humming through my dreams. I'd always wake just moments later to a huge red sun dawning on a vast horizon. A quick piss, a gulp of red wine, a hunk of cold apple pie, then down the cliffs into the surf. I was sixteen.

At twenty-eight, from the airplane, the surf was only white chalk marks outlining the borders of the land. Yet I had that same feeling of wonder, of suddenly waking from sleep, from a dream, to a bright new day. And this new day I was coming home.

Small towns passed beneath the plane. As our shadow touched them, the memories they held flowed up to me: Patchogue, where I went to high school; the Fire Island beaches I'd lifeguarded; the Great South Bay I'd fished as a kid; Babylon, my home. I was traveling back into my past and found myself crying softly for a time that was gone and a world that used to be.

I must have drifted off because I was sitting against a prison wall, staring at a morning sky, totally at peace with the world—when huge wheels skidded onto the runway with a jarring shock and the wind roared. We were on the ground, Kennedy Airport, good ole U.S. of A. The plane slowed and taxied toward the gate. I wondered what type of legality awaited me—after all, I was an escaped convict. I hoped it would be quick and I could avoid fingerprinting. I hated all that black ink on my hands.

As we filed out of the jet, I saw a man in a gray suit inquiring of the passengers, "Mr. Hayes? Mr. Hayes?" Ah, yes, the inevitable authorities. He seemed pleasant enough, shook my hand as I introduced myself. "Mr. Hayes? John Lauder."

"You're with the police, I assume?"

He laughed. "Oh, no, I work here—Pan Am representative. Welcome home. And congratulations. If you'll follow me, please."

Which I did, down some side stairs—didn't even go through customs, which I found rather ironic, all things considered. I even had a momentary thought of...No! No! stop thinking like that....

John led me down some side stairs, explaining, "Your father and brother and lawyer are waiting for you, and we thought it might be easier this way to avoid the crowds at customs." I wasn't quite sure what was happening, but I smiled and nodded my head and followed John.

At the end of a narrow corridor, he opened a pale green door. Dad was standing on the other side, his hair was all silver now, but the arms that held me were still strong, and the blue eyes shone with happiness. I reached out my arm and pulled my brother Rob to us, and he bear-hugged us all as I stood there weeping with joy, wrapped in the love and warmth of my family. I was starved for them, for their touch and the reassurance of home and blood.

My lawyer over the years, Michael Griffith, grabbed my hand and started pumping. There was a huge grin on his handsome face. "Welcome home, Billy!" As always, he looked like he slid off the cover of *GQ* magazine. "Damn it! I should be pissed at you. We had that transfer on our fingertips and you ruin it by escaping."

"Sorry to upset your plans, Michael."

"Jesus!" he laughed. "I'm so glad you made it. When we didn't hear any news after the escape, we got really worried. What happened after you got off the island?"

"That's a long story, and I'll need at least one cold beer."

Dad said, "Listen, Will, there are a few reporters upstairs waiting to talk to you." He looked at Michael. Mike had helped generate publicity when my original four-year sentence was changed to thirty years. He'd been working on a prisoner exchange treaty with Turkey when I escaped, and apparently he was still doing P.R. work. "Mike contacted them when we got your call from Amsterdam. You can talk with them if you like, or we can just slip out a side door. There's a car waiting, it won't be any trouble."

It really didn't matter to me if I spoke with the press or not. I was free. Whatever happened next was fine with me. "Talk to a few reporters?" I said. "Sure, why not? Hell, I'll talk to anybody. I'm free! What's a few guys with notepads?"

Dad told me about the family as we followed John down another corridor to a set of double doors. I could hear a deep murmuring on the other side. John pushed open the doors and led us into a large room jammed with people. The crowd noise rose as a path opened before us. Flashbulbs began popping. Glaring bright lights snapped on, and I was suddenly aware of TV cameras following my progress. Our pace increased. Rob was at my elbow, guiding me toward a table against the far wall where banks of microphones and tape recorders were set up. I was stunned by the size of "a few reporters." Dad sat down next to me behind the table. We were surrounded by a tight semicircle of faces, cameras, lights and equipment.

Mike quieted the press with a short introduction then asked for questions. Hands flew up from the crowd. Voices rang out.

"Billy, Billy, what's it feel like to be home?"

I laughed and looked at my watch. "I really don't know. I've only been here...two minutes. Haven't seen my mom."

"Did the CIA help you escape?"

"What!? God, no. Where were they? I would have loved a helicopter."

I'd been fiddling with something in my pocket and pulled out a large five-lira Turkish coin, which had somehow managed to make it back with me. Dad and I looked at each other, then he grinned. "Better hope you don't get a chance to spend *that* anytime soon."

"How'd you get from Turkey to Greece?"

"How do you feel about drug laws in this country?"

"What are your plans now?"

Photographers angled around on the ground while mouths moved in faces around me and arms waved in slow motion above the crowd. The noise, the press, the whole experience seemed surreal, bizarre—as if I were somehow a detached observer of the scene. I'd had the same feeling in an Istanbul courtroom as the judge sentenced me to life in prison, but that day I wasn't glowing with excitement, as I was now. Still, after five years of isolation, I wasn't ready for this sort of reception. I could handle it (after prison, what could be hard?), but I kept my arm around Dad's shoulder just to have a solid anchor.

A blonde woman up front had been staring at me. "Were you ever beaten in prison?"

"Yes, my first night."

"Would you describe it?"

"They tied my ankles with rope and beat my feet."

Her eyes were locked on mine. "Were you ever raped?"

I stared at her. Her interest was intense. I felt myself becoming aroused. A man said, "I believe a few of your prison letters were published in newspapers and that you were a writer in college. Do you plan on doing a book about your experience?"

I was glad the wall was behind me. In a crowd of strangers, I liked to keep my back covered—a prison habit I'd picked up after seeing a friend stabbed three times in the back at lunch one day. I took my eyes from the blonde and answered the man. "I don't know. I really don't know what I'll do. I'm healthy, alive and free. That's enough for me at the moment."

I don't remember walking from the press conference to the car. The soft afternoon sun hung hazy yellow, and the air smelled of fall as we cruised along the Southern State Parkway, heading for Babylon. We stopped for gas—the pump read 65 cents per gallon. It was 23 cents when I left. I leaned back and closed my eyes. Happiness was an immense glowing ball inside me, but I was almost afraid to open my eyes and find myself still in prison, dreaming of freedom as I'd done so many times before. This time, though, I knew it was real. With that odd sense of detachment, I looked at myself and realized that freedom meant more than leaving the stone walls behind. I felt free within myself. I'd learned something about my strengths and weaknesses, and I'd come to accept myself for who I was. I wasn't actually sure who I was, but I'd let that come with time. The opening words of my prison diary floated to mind: "To accept myself for who I am brings me peace; to strive to become the man I think I must drives me mad; I live in a state of peaceful madness..."

13

Peaceful Madness

Peaceful madness. It was an apt description of life since I'd returned. I was still sitting on the bench in Central Park, staring out at an empty lake—the ducks and swans were gone.

My first two weeks home had been wonderful, but not at all what I'd expected. I'd expected a very quiet return to the Outside. Quiet and simple. I'm really a simple kind of guy. Make me smile, fill my belly, tickle my balls—I'm happy.

For years, one of my prison fantasies had been of a deserted beach on the coast of Morocco, south of Rabat. Huddled under blankets on bitter winter nights, I'd dream of being free on this sun-drenched beach, alone and naked with a woman who just wanted to eat fruit, make love and swim in the ocean. It seemed fitting that there was now a huge political confrontation in Morocco—soldiers, guns, landmines, and 250,000 people marching across my deserted dream-beach. I got off the bench, lifted the bike and pedaled away, laughing at myself. Expectations. I'd learned about them long ago, but they were still leading me astray.

I cruised north into the lush foliage at the far end of the park. It reminded me of the trees and bushes around our house in Babylon, and how amazed I'd been to see their growth my first day home. I'd stepped from the car after the ride from the airport and saw one tree that I hardly remembered now towered over the front yard, and its roots had lifted and cracked the concrete driveway. Some waiting reporters began to ask questions, but I saw my mother standing by

the open screen door, her thin, sweet face beaming at the sight of her long-lost son, the years of pain flowing from her eyes. I crushed her in my arms.

The phone was ringing in the kitchen as we entered.

"Billy! Billy!" cried my tiny grandmother as I lifted her like a bird. "I prayed so hard for you to come home."

"Thanks, Nana, I needed all the help I could get."

"You're not home two minutes and already the phone is ringing off the hook." I hugged my sister, Peg, burying my face in her long blonde hair. She was a little girl when I left, and now she was a beautiful young woman. Incredible.

The phone kept ringing; friends, well-wishers, media requests for interviews. We took it off the hook to have some peace at dinner. Mom had cooked roast beef and baked an apple pie. Nana made a huge bowl of her famous rice pudding. I ate and talked and laughed so much I could barely breathe.

Then I was drying off after twenty ecstatic minutes under the hot shower when I heard Peg's excited shout from downstairs. "Billy! Dad! Hey, everybody! Look at this— we're on television." Sure enough, there we were—Dad and Rob and me at the airport press conference. We'd made the seven o'clock news on every station. It was strange enough just seeing a television, much less watching myself on it.

"Oh, Billy," said Mom, "you look so thin on TV."

"Feed him some more rice pudding," cackled Nana.

"But Dad looks great, doesn't he, Peg?"

"Right, Mom, especially the way his silver hair shines." Dad gave her a look. "You know, Billy, I always knew that someday you'd be famous."

The TV announcer was saying, "Billy Hayes returned this afternoon to a hero's welcome at Kennedy Airport. Hayes, 28, escaped from an Istanbul prison after serving five years of a thirty-year sentence for attempting to smuggle four pounds of hashish out of Turkey..."

"Peg," I said, "I think the word is infamous."

It was a rather ironic pun. Vain and egotistical, I guess I'd always sought recognition. Now I was suddenly known to millions, but as an escaped, convicted drug smuggler—not exactly the best aspects of my personality. Since it was true, I'd have to accept it, but then I didn't know what to make of this hero stuff. Escaping from prison was big news for the media, but for me it was the end of a long and desperate struggle just to get back to even, to stop the daily pain I'd created for myself and those innocent people who loved me. I was proud that I'd survived and escaped prison; I wasn't proud of the actions that had gotten me there.

Seeing myself on TV was the perfect ending to a bizarre, exhausting day. Mom had fixed up my old room and lovingly tucked me into bed.

"Your old room," she said, tears welling in her eyes. Then she laughed and hugged me. "I'm just so happy, it's like a miracle."

"I love you, Mom."

"I love you, Billy, sleep well."

She closed the door. I gazed around at photos and banners tacked to the walls, high school yearbooks, trophies and mementos of another life piled on shelves. I clicked off the light and fell into a deep, dreamless sleep.

14

Marc and Melissa

The next morning a spinning Turkish coin glinted in the rays of the dawning sun. I caught it in my palm and pressed it flat against the cool smooth bark of the towering elm tree that had so magically appeared in the front yard. I heard the screen door open behind me.

"Sorry, Mom, did I wake you?" My breath steamed the chilly air. She closed her robe at the throat. "No, it's all right. You know how I sleep." She looked at the hammer and big three-penny nail in my right hand but only said, "I thought you might be going fishing, like you used to."

"Not today," I said, feeling only slightly foolish. "Got something to do." She watched as I pressed the point of the nail into the center of the coin. I tapped it softly a few times then drove it home, deeply embedding the metal disc into the wood. Mom came up beside me and slowly rubbed her fingers over the coin, the broken bark. "Won't take this tree long to heal," she said, "it's got good roots."

"You're still corny," I said, putting my arm around her thin shoulders.

"You nail a coin into a tree and I'm corny?"

We stood together awhile, listening to the gentle October morning.

We left the phone off the hook most of that first weekend. Saturday night a party had been planned for Nana's 80th birthday,

65

so I got to see all my relatives in one shot. I woke up Sunday morning with my face sore from grinning.

We were gathered around the breakfast table in robes and slippers, sipping our coffee and reading the papers, when a strange, trumpet-like horn sounded outside. "I'll get it," said Dad, who'd been up for hours and already completed two games of handball. He drew back the curtains on the front window then let out a low whistle. "Hey, Will, I think this must be for you."

A sleek white Rolls Royce Silver Cloud was idling softly, purring in the driveway. Sunlight glinted off the windshield, obscuring my view, but I had few doubts who was driving this old classic. I was halfway to the car before the door flew open—he always loved the dramatic flair. Marc (Dr. Muskrat) bounded out and planted his short, powerful frame on the lawn in front of me, assuming the familiar wrestling stance of our high school days. His eyes glittered beneath bushy brows, and his dark, pointed goatee was parted by a mischievous grin. I hadn't seen Marc since a prison visit in 1972. He was a weirdly wonderful dynamo of energy, the one corner of my high school triumvirate—Marc, Norman and me. We traveled Europe together on a motorcycle in the Sixties and ran with the bulls in Pamplona. We faced each other a moment, then reached out and clasped forearms in that silly Roman soldier embrace we'd somehow adopted. He looked at me with joy and wonder...and something else. I wasn't sure what it was. I knew by the tone of his last letters that it had been hard for him being Outside all these years, wanting to help but unable to do much. He tried to speak but it wasn't necessary. I laughed and spread my arms in mock wonder at the car. He beamed and opened the back door. The interior was thick carpeting, gleaming chrome and smooth walnut panels. The plush tan leather seats caressed me as I folded back into them. A panel slid open, and I looked up into a huge pair of brown eyes as a lovely lady leaned through the partition from the front with a silver tray extended, champagne and glasses sparkling.

"Welcome home, Billy. I'm Melissa. Champagne?"

The three of us drank a quick toast to my return, then Marc had to run—late, late, for a very important date—and we agreed to meet soon at his auto showroom in Great Neck.

15

Floating Fantasy

That evening, Mike Griffith took Rob and me to a huge party at a mansion in Southampton. Laughter and music floated out to us as we approached the hip crowd partying on the sprawling lawn. Mike led us through the crowd, glad-handing everyone, making introductions, gathering people around us like filings to a magnet. My social awkwardness was heightened by my sudden notoriety, most everyone having seen me on TV or in the newspapers. Heads turned as I passed, comments whispered behind raised hands. I quickly became the center of attention and felt like Marco Polo just come back from the Mysterious East. I felt a strange ambivalence—in prison I avoided attracting attention, now I was feeding on it.

I looked around and saw Rob staring at the foxy women and posh surroundings. He nodded to the sky, and I followed his glance to a towering hot air balloon that hung above the yard on a long tether rope—a toy for the guests' amusement. We burst out laughing. I excused myself from the group and walked with Rob down to the sand dunes beside the ocean. Waves broke along the shoreline while the sounds of the party tinkled in the background.

"I feel like fucking Marco Polo," I said.

Rob nodded at the house. "Well, Marco, this isn't too bad for your third night home."

"It beats prison by a long shot."

"So, what's next?" he asked.

I stared out at the dark ocean. "Good question. What is next? I hadn't planned much beyond getting out."

"You gonna write this book?"

"Sure got enough offers," I said, skimming a stone across the water.

Rob looked at me. "But you don't want to."

"I don't know. Maybe later. I'm not sure I want to spend my time out here thinking about back there. But I've got to do something about money."

"And it isn't smuggling," said my brother, with a smile.

"That's right," I grinned.

"Which leaves you with what—lifeguard?"

I burst out laughing. "I wish I could, but you know how much I owe everyone, Dad with the second on the house..."

"Don't worry about it, we're all okay."

"I know that, it's just...I'm tired of owing everybody."

"Well, like you say, whatever you do will beat prison by a long shot. You know my couch in Manhattan is yours for as long as you want. Even got a new Remington typewriter."

I reached out and hugged my brother, lifting him off the sand. "I'm so happy to see you!"

He lifted me off the sand. "And I'm so happy to have you home!"

Back at the mansion a crowd quickly gathered around me, and the subject, invariably, came around to sex in prison. I was feeling rather awkward, when a dark-haired woman in a sheer white dress deftly separated me from the crowd and led me out back toward the balloon.

"I'm Mona," she said. "I own all this."

"I'm impressed," I said, staring at the house and her cleavage.

We climbed into the wicker basket, then a whooshing burst of flame from the overhead gas burner gently lifted us off the grass. We rose into the dark night sky and hovered above the brightly lit house at the end of a long rope tether. I gazed around in wonder, once again a child at the fair. Mona smiled at me a moment, then slowly raised her white dress above her thighs, revealing her nakedness. I was dumbstruck. She slowly fondled herself with one hand and gave the balloon a blast of hot air with the other. It strained against the tether. She dropped to her knees before me. There was a moment of fear, an awareness of the people below that quickly faded as the pleasure overwhelmed me and I exploded, laughing and crying into the night.

16

A Difficult Visit

Monday morning I sat at the kitchen table and began taking phone calls. Dad and Rob stayed home to help, Mom scrambled eggs and poured coffee, Nana plied me with rice pudding. By noon we had a three-page list of requests for interviews. Mike Griffith felt it essential to act while media interest was high, and had set up a series of meetings with enthusiastic literary agents. At some point that first weekend, I'd decided to write a book. I wasn't totally comfortable with the idea—I wanted to forget prison, not write about it—but the decision was economic. My father had taken a second mortgage on the family home to support me in prison. I'd come back $25,000 in debt with no money or job, and employment prospects looked dim: "My previous employment? Ah, convict." That would get me a lot of work.

I needed a break after lunch and took my dad's Volvo out for a drive around the neighborhood. I found myself cruising slowly, bicycle speed, down well-remembered streets. Then the car stopped and I was looking at a trim white Cape Cod house with green shutters. A huge hedge grew beside the driveway, and for an instant, I thought there was a rusting black Morgan sports car sitting up on blocks. Then it was gone.

Norman and I used to sit for hours in that classic old car on the blocks, weaving boyhood dreams of worlds without end. He bought the Morgan cheap when we were sixteen, towed it home, and set it on blocks to be repaired. It never came down.

But the car was gone now, as was Norman. He'd been so excited that last day he'd visited me in prison in Istanbul. His green eyes shone, and I could feel him right through the glass partition. He had come, like a true friend, to help me escape. I had thought I could escape by returning to the madhouse, Bakirkoy Mental Hospital, only this time with reliable help waiting outside the walls with a car, money, clothes and papers. We discussed strategy, then Norman left, grinning like a leprechaun. He went back to Mannheim, Germany, where he'd gotten a job in the John Deere tractor factory, making money and arranging false passports for the escape. For Norman, a singer of Irish ballads and writer of romantic poetry, this was an adventure rivaling *The Count of Monte Cristo*. Until someone put a bayonet through his chest in a dingy hotel room.

I left the Volvo and walked slowly up the empty driveway toward the house. I checked an impulse to whistle at the upper window, which made me sad. Norman's younger brother, Brian, responded to my knock. He'd gotten bigger, filled out. A variety of emotions flashed across his handsome face, then he shook my hand and pulled me into the living room. Mr. Shaw was in his customary chair, feet propped on a hassock, reading as usual. Norman's love for books had come from his father. He set his wine glass on the table and peered at me over the black rim of his spectacles.

"Well, I'll be...Nan!" he called out to the kitchen, "Nan, guess who's here?"

I heard Mrs. Shaw's muffled response.

"Welcome home, Billy," he said, his face breaking into a smile. "It's been a long time."

"Oh, my God! Billy! Billy!" cried Mrs. Shaw, rushing out of the kitchen to hug me. "I'm so glad you're home. We read about it and saw the TV. Your folks must be so happy."

"Yes, they are. Thanks."

"Sit down, sit down. Brian, get Billy some wine."

"No, thanks," I said, "I can only stay a moment. I don't want to intrude." I'd known these people most of my life but felt like a stranger, an unwanted guest.

"Don't be silly," she said, motioning Brian to bring the wine. "We haven't seen you in years. Sit, talk with us." She led me to the couch.

"I was just in the neighborhood..." I said, so lamely that we all laughed. My throat was suddenly dry. I sipped some wine. "I feel so bad about Norman," I started, then stopped to hold back a sob. Mrs. Shaw's face broke for a moment, and I felt so terribly guilty being there while her son lay buried in the cold German ground.

She took a deep breath and patted my hand. "I know you do. We all do. Such a waste."

"He was there because of me, so I feel responsible—"

"He was there because he loved you."

Mr. Shaw said, "We're all responsible, including Norman, so don't eat yourself up."

We all talked for a while, taking comfort in each other and the sharing of our common loss. Then it was time to leave.

Mrs. Shaw smiled at me. "We're so happy for you. Give your folks our love and come back soon, you hear? Having you here makes me think he'll come bounding down the stairs any moment now. You guys are always together in my mind."

I knew what she meant. I still couldn't picture a world without the possibility of Norman's smiling face suddenly appearing around some unexpected corner.

17

A Strange Bitter Taste

The bike vibrated on some rough pavement and brought me back to Central Park; the memory bubble of Norman burst and disappeared. There were a lot of memory bubbles percolating in my mind now that I was writing. The money from a book advance would relieve my immediate financial problems, but it meant I'd have to spend the next year reliving the prison experience on paper. I wasn't sure I was ready for that, but it seemed a bit late for second thoughts as I pedaled out into the street traffic heading for my meeting with Julian.

Bright sunlight slanted in through the high, arched windows of Julian's office. We were just off Fifth Avenue, but the traffic noise was muffled, the high-ceilinged room cozy and littered with books, boxes, and stacks of paper. I sat in an armchair watching the floating dust motes while Julian reviewed the outline and first fifteen pages of *Midnight Express*. He wanted some idea of my style and approach; I wanted his approval. I hoped to use these pages to sway a desperately needed advance from an obliging publisher.

Julian removed his glasses and pinched the bridge of his aristocratic nose. "Well, Billy, this is very good for one reason. Now we know we'll need a professional writer."

"What?"

"You write like you speak—scattered, in a running stream of consciousness. The 'hysterical subjective,' I might call it."

"So, what's wrong with that style to tell my story?"

"Nothing, if you're happy communicating only with your immediate peers. We could publish it in *Rolling Stone*, perhaps, but if you want to reach beyond that audience—and to make any money from this we must reach beyond—then we'll need a professional writer to work with you, organize and direct you."

I was crushed. I was also relieved. I'd committed myself to this book but didn't know if I could do it—didn't know if I really wanted to do it. I wanted to forget prison, not write about it; at least not yet, not so soon. But I needed the money and wanted to say "I'm writing a book," to all the questions people kept asking me about my future plans. I wanted to write it myself, yet from the first efforts, I realized that the jumble of characters, events, and emotions was overwhelming. It felt like it was a moral compromise to accept a co-author, but I wanted help organizing and trying to make sense of the prison years.

"What do you have in mind?" I asked.

"Let me set up some meetings for you with writers I know," said Julian. "Meanwhile, you keep churning out that raw verbiage—it's good, powerful and expressive. Maybe you could work with a tape recorder. And be aware of reader empathy and the negative commercial aspects of your story. We're dealing with subjects that might easily offend large segments of potential readers—prison, drugs, homosexuality. You're a semi-famous escaped convict now, but we have to make them realize you were just a dumb kid then, who made one big mistake that almost cost him his life."

"There's no doubt I was dumb—the actions and consequences speak for themselves—but what do you mean by 'one big mistake'? The fact that I was caught?"

"The fact that you tried to smuggle hash at all was your one big mistake."

I watched the dust motes floating through a sunbeam. "Do you think it would affect things if this hadn't been the first time I'd smuggled hash?"

Julian stared at me a moment. "I think," he said slowly, "it might affect things a great deal. I think it might ruin everything."

So…

I'd been arrested in October 1970, trying to smuggle two kilos of hashish onto an airplane at the Istanbul airport. Hoping to receive a lighter sentence, I told the Turkish court that I intended the hash for my own use, not for sale. They didn't ask me if this was my first smuggling attempt, and I didn't volunteer any information. The court, the American Consul, my lawyers, everyone involved, just assumed this was my first attempt at smuggling. It wasn't. For my own benefit, I let the assumption stand. It immediately became a lie.

In order for other people to believe the lie, I had to believe it. So I did. From that point on, this was my first smuggling attempt. No one doubted it. I said it so long it almost became true. But not quite. A lie is a clinging thing—the longer you nurture and feed its growth, the stronger its hold on you. By the time I escaped in 1975, the lie was already part of a media image of me—and as I expanded, the lie expanded. I didn't have the courage to kill it, and while admitting the truth could have serious legal consequences here at home, it still felt like a moral cowardice. It was easier to tell interviewers the partial truth when they asked why I went to Turkey—"I was out of college, wandering around Europe, running out of money, and it seemed like a good idea at the time." A partial truth is worse than an honest-to-God lie. It's an act of omission, a snivel rather than a roar.

I stared at Julian and said nothing. After a moment he stood up and walked to the window, talking again about advances and media interest. "There are some editors I want you to meet, tell your story. These TV and radio interviews are good for publicity, but I don't think we should do any more. Not now. Later, when the book comes out. And don't spill the entire tale. Remember, every word out of your mouth may be a dollar out of your pocket."

I listened as his words floated with the dust motes in the quiet room, and a strange, bitter taste slowly filled my mouth. I know a moral compromise when I taste one.

I tried to rationalize my feelings, but it was too late; something had shifted inside me, and that sense of purity I'd had since escaping was gone.

18

It Cuts Both Ways

Every word out of my mouth a dollar out of my pocket? Christ! If that was true, I'd already lost thousands since I'd been home. Rob's bike had a flat tire when I left Julian's office, so I found myself clinging to a ceiling-strap as the crowded subway rumbled towards 14th Street. Julian's statement made me wonder about the true value of my words. People were suddenly interested in me. Thirty days ago I was in prison eating beans, and now I was being seen on TV, heard on radio, and read about in newspapers. For five years my big media event had been mail call three times a week; now I was a media event. Very interesting transition.

At 42nd Street the subway doors slid open as a human tide washed out then poured back in again. As usual, I was feeling ambiguous about crowds, and the bicycle was awkward, but the press of bodies was exciting in the sweet stale air. I found myself standing directly above a pretty Spanish girl who sat reading *Cosmopolitan*. Her white blouse was open at the throat. I stared down at the delicate bones of her shoulders and the small, creamy mounds of her breasts. I felt my erection stiffen and shift in my sweatpants. It was suddenly terribly urgent for me to have her hand caress my bulging crotch. We were only inches apart. I willed her to look up, to raise her eyes and see my longing so near her crimson lips. I closed my eyes and imagined her fingers sliding up my thigh. The lights flickered as the train rattled around a turn; the crowd swayed and I accidentally brushed myself against the back of her hand. I pulled back instantly. Her angry eyes snapped to my startled face as the train shuddered to a stop and she quickly jostled her way out the door.

I was more than embarrassed, I was infuriated with myself for letting that happen. I constantly fantasized about the endless stream of women flowing around me in New York, but I'd let a fantasy get out of control. God! I had to be careful. I couldn't just reach out and touch any woman who aroused me on the street, particularly since I felt as randy as a three-balled billy goat. For years I'd reached out for women, but they'd always been in my dreams; to have so many so near now still felt like a dream. I always did have trouble defining reality.

Some black teenagers piled into the car, laughing and jiving around. I noticed a big kid with cornrow hair checking me out. "Yo," he said, "ain't you the dude on TV last week, guy bust out that prison?"

I nodded and smiled, hoping he'd drop it, but his face lit up as he turned to his friends. "Yo, Wallace, Mookie, hey, check it out— this the dude from the news!"

Mookie, slightly zonked and cross-eyed, stepped up close to stare in my face.

"Where the fuck was that?" asked Cornrow.

"Turkey," I replied softly, aware of the other passengers tuning in to the conversation.

"Turkeey!" shouted Mookie, suddenly animated. "Thas right, the dude wit da hasheesh!" He reached out and did a series of moves on my extended hand. I was getting very uncomfortable.

"Yeah," said Cornrow, grinning, "That's some rare shit I been readin' about you in the papers."

"It's been a weird trip," I said, as the train braked and everyone swayed forward. Cornrow raised his fist and shouted "Way to go, Whiteboy!" as the surging crowd swept me out the open door. I heard Mookie singing "Hasheee—esh! Hasheee—esh!" as the doors closed and the train pulled away.

I held onto the bicycle, waiting for the crowd to pass. There was a tug at my sleeve, and I recognized a small dark woman with intense eyes who'd been staring at me on the subway.

"I just want you to know," she said, fixing me with her sorrowful gaze, "that my daughter died from a drug overdose, and I think you're a piece of shit." Then she carefully spit on my pants, turned, and slowly walked away.

19

Fever Dreams

I was on the couch watching the evening news when Rob came home from work. He dropped a pizza on the table and tossed a magazine on my chest. "Seen this yet?" he asked, heading into the bedroom to change out of his suit. I looked at a picture of Bob Dylan on the cover of *People* magazine. "How'd your meeting go with Julian?"

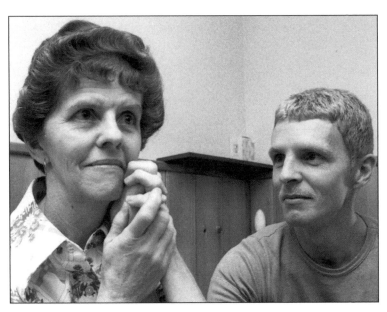

Photo by Harry Benson

"All right," I said distractedly, turning pages. There we were—Mom and I sitting on my bed in Babylon, hugging each other and smiling gamely for the camera. The accompanying story was the now-familiar rehash of my escape.

"So he liked your writing," said Rob, crossing to the kitchen, popping a beer. My brother hadn't changed much in five years—some gray now in his short brown hair, but fit and healthy, with the legs that had won him a soccer scholarship to Brown University still muscled from miles of biking.

"So," Rob repeated, "he liked your writing?"

"What? Oh, no, not exactly." I explained the situation.

"Interesting," said my brother, knowing me well.

Yes. Very interesting. Interesting was my favorite adjective these days. It was the only word that seemed to cover the full breadth of the prison experience—an experience that was continuing, I realized, beyond the bars and in ways I'd never imagined. We dug into the pizza then settled back to watch *Young Frankenstein* on cable TV.

I was standing barefoot on the cold stone prison floor, staring down at a restless figure asleep on his bunk...he was twisting and turning, his face was sweating...I realized it was me...the figure sat bolt upright as if waking from a nightmare and stared at me.

I woke and heard the late night sounds of New York out the window. My heart was racing, I was covered in sweat. There wasn't much point in sleep anymore, so I dressed and took Rob's Volvo out for a cruise.

I slowly drove the quiet streets until I found myself on the West Side, near the abandoned piers along the Hudson River. The streets were lined with hookers—slinky good lookers of both sexes and several indeterminates, all bold and proud of their strutting bodies. I stopped at a corner, and a brown girl in black leather sauntered over and tapped on my window with long silver fingernails. She leaned in when I lowered the window, her coat opening to some great cleavage. "Looking for a date, Mister?"

"I can't sleep," I said, reaching for my crotch.

"I can see why," she said, scraping a silver nail along my jeans. She looked at my short hair. "You ain't a cop, are you, honey?"

That made me laugh. "Not even close."

"You got cop eyes."

"Maybe I just seen too many of 'em."

She looked at me a moment. "So what you want?"

"Some head."

"Twenty dollars."

"Where?"

She looked at me again. "Where? Right here in the car, unless you wanna get a room."

"Right here on the street?" This talk of cops was making me nervous.

"No," she said, "Over there by the water. Nobody bother us there." She slid her leathered legs into the passenger seat. "You new around here, baby?"

"Sort of," I said, slipping her a twenty and heading for the docks.

20

Barbara

Ten o'clock on a bright November morning, my running shoes were puma pads and I was a young cat sniffing the breeze as I swiftly weaved the crowded sidewalks on my way across town. I'd been up for hours, done my yoga, written almost two pages and now skipped off the curb into the bustling traffic on 8th Avenue in front of Port Authority Bus Terminal. Barbara *[I called her Lillian in Midnight Express]* had called a few days ago from some truck stop in the Midwest. She'd been hiking in the mountains of British Columbia and had just heard the news of my escape.

Barbara had been my high school friend, sometimes lover and kindred spirit, who became my eyes while I was Inside. Her letters had offered desperately needed touches of femininity in a cold, masculine world. They'd sustained me when I woke from gray granite dreams, numbed and suffocating from the weight of empty years stretching out in both directions. I used to reach out and touch the envelopes she'd touched; trace my fingers along the thin flowing script; feel her in the paper. She'd float down into my darkness like a tiny glowing light that grew with my growing awareness of it. Lines of words became lines of thought, and thought bridged the distance between us. Energy would flow, and I'd find the strength to go on.

Her bus was due at ten-thirty. Port Authority was mobbed. I threaded my way into the noisy, shuffling throng and skirted around two of New York's Finest, rocking on their heels in the doorway. I passed a grubby wino who reminded me of a Turkish beggar and had the amusing thought that I was entering the covered bazaar of Istanbul.

I bought a copy of the *Times* and a Baby Ruth bar before following the signs downstairs toward Gate 29. The grimy tile corridors were brightly lit, crowded and noisy with diesel motors rumbling in the darkness beyond thick glass windows. The benches at Gate 29 were full, so I squatted on my heels Turkish style in a corner and quickly scanned the room over the top of the paper. Young black kid—thin, looks fast, friendly, no threat. Older balding man—stocky, powerful, tools hanging from belt, potential danger but harmless. Two Hispanic teenagers—restless, pacing the room, no problem, but note their movements. I did this sort of thing automatically; I liked to know where alternate exits and fire doors were. I didn't allow it to cramp my style, but being careful made me comfortable.

Two old Italian ladies in black sat mumbling to each other. I gave them a thick-bodied, middle-aged daughter, returning home now that her husband had run off with his secretary. A pale, mousey girl with dirty ankles crossed her shapely legs, and I could feel the weight of her thin body in my hands as I lifted her onto my lap. A sad young black woman in shabby clothes sat with quiet dignity staring at her reflection in the dirty glass. She was motionless, except for her arm that moved like a leash with a frisky little boy frolicking at the end. I had her waiting for a man and knew he wasn't worthy of her strength and patience.

I took a small bite of candy and shifted it to the left side of my mouth. That was the side I chewed with this week. The right side was under construction, the beginning of a major dental overhaul—twelve crowns and five replacement teeth for the ones lost in prison. My newly acquired dentist, Ron Rosen, would be proud of me—only chewing candy on the good side. He'd seen the airport press conference on TV and had heard me tell reporters about bad teeth being the worst physical effect of prison. I explained my unpleasant economic situation when he first phoned the house in Babylon, but he wasn't concerned with money. He had me stop by his office and examined my mouth. He was brisk and cheerfully efficient and let out several low whistles of appreciation as he spotted gnarly dental peculiarities.

"Tell you what," he said, leaning back and switching off the light, "I'll take it as a personal challenge to repair your teeth, do it for nothing in the early mornings before office hours." This was a very generous offer. "All you have to do is open wide and tell me your story. I'm fascinated by it. I had relatives in the camps."

Well, Turkish prison in no way compared to the Nazi camps, but I was willing to talk if Ron was willing to fix my teeth. "Let's start right away," he said, surprising me.

I gulped and nodded.

"Would you like gas?" he asked.

"Yes," I answered. "What is gas?"

"Nitrous oxide—you float away on it." He slipped a little plastic breathing piece over my nose. I took some deep breaths and relaxed back into the chair. From a hollow distance I heard Ron ask if they had gas in Turkey...in Turkey...in Turkey...and I remembered when I first felt the dull thumping in my back molar on a Friday morning, two months after being arrested. My Belgian friend, Johann, placed three blue capsules in my hand and informed me that the civilian dentist visits the prison on Mondays. A capsule a day was my only help till then.

My slowly throbbing tooth kept time with the agonizing minutes as they dragged their way through the weekend. Monday morning, a small, goofy guard named Latif opened the cellblock door, accepted the customary pack of cigarettes bribe, and led me to the hospital cellblock on the other side of the prison. He placed me in an old, cracked leather dentist chair set up in an empty room and told me to wait. This was getting scary. A beating wasn't fun, but at least it was external; this was internal and intimate and there was a matter of trust involved. I heard some coarse laughing and coughing, opened my eyes. Even through the Nembutal blur and the blinding pain of my toothache, I knew it was a bad sign when the wheezened Armenian dentist hung his apparatus from a hook in the ceiling and began pumping the foot pedal of his tarnished metal drill. The bright steel point whirred, emitting a high pitched little scream that seemed to satisfy him. He smiled, greeted me in Turkish then asked, I assumed, "Where does it hurt?" I opened reluctantly and pointed to the back molar. He placed the small mirror in my mouth and leaned down over me, one eye squinting and watering, the other squeezed shut to avoid the smoke curling up from a home-made cigarette that dangled from his old, cracked lips. He poked around, muttering to himself, humming some atonal nasal tune, then tapped the molar once. I rose up off chair. "Yes, yes," he said, confirming his own judgment. He pumped the pedal a few times, revving the drill, then motioned for me to open wide...

"You can sit up now," said Ron, after that first visit. I'd been aware of his activity on my teeth, but I just hadn't cared. "So you liked the gas?" he asked.

"Float me away like that, you can take all my teeth out."

He laughed. "How about six in the morning, Monday, Wednesday, and Friday for a couple of weeks?"

That's what I'd been doing, and it was such a relief not to have a toothache that I ate the last bite of candy to celebrate my dental recuperation.

I stood and stretched when I heard the bus approaching. Headlights cut an arc through the darkness, and the crowd rose as a huge rumbling machine slid into Gate 29 and stopped inches from the glass. Barbara stepped off the bus—faded jeans, baggy gray sweater, long brown hair and the shyest of smiles.

I held her in my arms as I'd held her in my dreams, but now the warm throbbing body was real, and the soft murmured words were from her lips, not my imagination. We gazed at each other from arm's length, my lonely years reflected in her eyes. I felt my own tears welling up but they were cleansing tears, tender tears, tears of joy.

She grabbed a small suitcase while I hefted her duffle bag onto my shoulder. Barbara traveled like she lived—light and simple, no frills. Her hand was in mine as we climbed the stairs. It was thin and strong with long-boned fingers, rough now from working manual jobs in strange places around the world. One day, years ago, Barbara had ventured out in search of something. She'd roamed forests, climbed mountains and slept beneath the

open skies; she'd rejected society's dictates and strove to find her own values. She'd looked from Alaska to Afghanistan, and for all that she'd found, I knew she was still looking now, in my eyes, as the rattling taxi bullied its way into traffic and headed downtown.

We lay in bed, exhausted, rapt in each other's arms. It had been powerful loving, but I'd been nervous and rushed things. At one point Barbara had held my face in her hands and whispered, "Slow, baby, go slow and easy," but I was still unsure of myself, and my fear of failure drove me on. I reached a frenzy and exploded inside her with a shuddering scream, then we both lay still while Barbara softly stroked the back of my neck.

"I'm crying," she said, as I licked a tear from her cheek. "I'm so happy, I'm crying."

I pushed back on my arms and looked down on her wet, beaming face. I traced my breath along her brow, all matted now with dark heavy hair, and softly blew her eyelids shut. I traced the thin line of nose and breathed on her full, quivering lips till they parted to draw me down inside her where the deep fire burned.

We slept on blankets on the floor that night, then caught the six a.m. train for Long Island. I had another dentist appointment in East Meadow with Ron Rosen, and Barbara was continuing to her folk's place in Babylon. Just before leaving I put some grass in a pipe and lit it.

"You smoke grass first thing in the morning?" Barbara asked, declining the pipe.

"I'm going to the dentist. Me and pain don't get along."

"What about Novocain?"

"What about it?"

"Nothing," laughed Barbara, lifting her suitcase. "I see you've learned a lot from getting busted." She saw the look on my face. "Oh, God, I'm sorry. You know what I mean."

"Yes," I smiled, "I know what you mean." We clasped hands and headed out into the streets.

The excitement of being with her made the morning train ride seem like one of the high school adventures we'd shared back in another lifetime. We'd stare at each other, unspeaking, for long moments, then both pour out endless streams of consciousness that mixed and merged and made magic connections between us. We agreed to meet again in the city in a few days.

21

Marc and the Bizarrini

After the dentist I took a cab to Marc's auto dealership in Great Neck. The lot was full of sparkling new Hondas, but inside the large showroom were several exotic- looking machines. I declined the help of an enthusiastic young salesman and wandered over to a low-slung silver monster.

"That's a twelve-cylinder Bizarrini," a familiar voice said behind me. "It seems to be just your style, sir."

I smiled and slid through the open door into the smooth leather embrace of the interior. "Vrroomm, vrrooomm. I might have to take this baby out for a spin. Where are the keys?"

Marc's dark eyes twinkled as he leaned down into the window. "Riiight. The keys. An escaped convict with no fucking license wants the keys to an $80,000 bat-outta-hell automobile." He stared at me a moment, then we embraced through the window. "Welcome back, man."

His office was a partitioned corner of the showroom with a tinted plate glass window facing the floor. It was all wood panels with a thick carpet, a large desk, a small kitchen bar and photos of classic sports cars covering the walls. Marc dumped some white powder on the bar and began chopping it with a razor blade.

"So what's the automobile business like these days?" I asked, leaning back in his black leather chair.

He continued to chop, then tilted his head and grinned. "You want to know about the automobile business? See the glass in front

of you? One way." That's right, I remembered it was opaque from the outside. "Open the right-hand desk drawer." I whistled low at the ugly snub-nosed .38 curled among some papers. "Now reach under the desk above your right knee." Jesus! There was a ten-inch bayonet taped underneath in its sheath.

"Marc, what's the story here? This feels like prison." He cut the coke into four long lines. "Just tools of the trade, my friend. Things are pretty crazy out here, too." He leaned down over the bar, sucked up two lines. "Forget the Sixties, man, they're over. You went away, bells were ringing in the air. This is the Seventies." He offered me the rolled-up hundred-dollar bill.

I stared at the bar. "I've never seen this shit before."

He grinned. "Trust me, you'll like it..."

I told Marc about my decision to write a book, and about the reservations I was feeling.

"So write a book, you'd be crazy not to. What else are you going to do for money, smuggle hash?"

"No. Smuggling's not exactly my style these days."

"That's your style," he said, indicating the Bizarrini, "But it takes a lot of bread." Marc had always worked hard and had money.

He'd been dealing in high-priced sports cars for years, but now the lot was full of Hondas.

"What's with all the Hondas? I thought you dealt in classy merchandise?"

Built low and powerful like the Bizarrini, he paced the office. "I'll tell you what I found out. Rich people are rich because they don't pay. They buy a car, and their check is cancelled before you get to the bank. Fuck 'em. What I say these days is: You sell to the classes, you sleep with the masses; you sell to the masses, you sleep with the classes. Hence, Hondas." He was humming like a dynamo.

"In fact, why don't you take one of those Hondas until you get some real wheels."

His offer wasn't surprising, but it touched me all the same. Marc had been lending me cars since high school.

"How about I drive the Bizarrini for a few weeks?"

He grinned and shook his head. "You couldn't get it out of second gear."

"Why not?"

"Because it does a hundred in second gear, and around here you'd kill yourself trying."

The Novocain was wearing off, my mouth began to ache. Marc insisted I take a thousand in cash, and I was truly grateful for the little blue Honda he lent me as I headed back toward Manhattan.

22

A Last Glimpse of Her Long Brown Hair

The following week Melissa invited Barbara and me over to dinner. We announced ourselves to the doorman in the lobby then hit the elevator button for the 21st floor. The gleaming metal doors slid closed with a hush. I pressed Barbara against the wall, and her hands were circling my ass when the bell rang again and the door opened on two little old ladies. We quickly separated and smiled at them. Barbara sputtered a short sound as my hidden fingers nudged her fancy. "Oh, excuse me," she said, stepping on my toe and twisting away. We kept straight faces to 21, then collapsed off the elevator in laughter.

Marc and Melissa lived high above the streets of Manhattan in a glass-fronted apartment with a magnificent view. "It's what keeps me from going crazy," said Melissa, indicating the dark, airy distance beyond the windows and the twinkling city below. "This is my quiet cave above the arena. Hi, Barbara, I'm Melissa." She kissed me on the cheek and accepted my bottle of wine. "Chateau Mouton. Nice. Your taste in wine is as good as your taste in women." I smiled at Barbara who'd selected the bottle. "Or perhaps," I said, "my women have as fine a taste for wine as they do for men."

Marc, corkscrew in hand, took the bottle from Melissa and said, "Then perhaps we should drink it rather than bullshit about it."

We feasted on Melissa's duck l'orange dinner, and the conversation soon turned to lifestyles and the relative merits of city versus country living. I was amused by the contrast between Melissa, who'd grown up on a farm and was now a sophisticated businesswoman working for a high-powered cosmetics company, and Barbara, who'd grown up in New York but now preferred a simpler life and quiet surroundings.

"Country people are so honest and simple," said Barbara, "less aggressive."

"Right," agreed Melissa. "It's that lack of ambition that allows them to settle for less."

"This broccoli is delicious," I said. "Anyone care for more?"

Melissa smiled. "I always want more."

"It's so easy to get distracted and lose your sense of values in a place like New York," said Barbara, looking at me.

"So I guess you're not planning to stay long," said Melissa, clearing the dishes into the kitchen.

"I'm not sure," said Barbara, smiling at me and surprising Marc by taking a small hit off the circulating joint. "I came to see Billy. A lot depends on him."

"Well," said Melissa, accepting the joint with a laugh, "New York is certainly not for the meek. But it looks like Billy, Marc and I are gonna be here for a spell, so if you ever make it back from the wilds, be sure to call, and the four of us'll have another lovely dinner."

Barbara knew I wanted to finish the book and stay here near my family. Being the media's latest mini-celebrity meant a dizzying increase in the pace of life, and Barbara knew I hungered for the excitement of New York after the stagnation of prison. She also knew something I was only beginning to realize—our long distance relationship of late-night love letters was over. We loved and were lovers, but our lives were moving in different directions, and the common dream of freedom that had bound us together was now forcing us apart. Barbara was calm and clear and knew what she wanted from life. I was crazed and confused by strange, new images of myself and intoxicated by the seemingly limitless horizons before me.

Barbara would have left her mountains and lived in the city if that was all our relationship needed. I wanted her to live with me and somehow repay her for being there through all the lonely years. But she knew how the lack of privacy in prison nearly drove me mad. In the cab home from Melissa's we rode in silence, each aware of the diverging paths before us.

"I guess you'll be needing a new wardrobe for the interviews and social scene. Melissa should be a big help with that."

I took her hand and said nothing as the cab rumbled down 2nd Avenue.

"You'll probably be real busy the next few months, what with the book and all, so I was thinking maybe I'd go back to the mountains for a while, take care of some loose ends, give you some space. Maybe come back in the spring."

I was confused. If I loved this woman I should ask her to stay, but then why was I flooded with relief at the thought of her leaving?

I hesitated, and the confusion on my face told her much more than the words that followed.

I started to speak, but she pressed a finger to my lips and said, "Shhh. It's all right. Things don't always work out the way we plan."

A week later we sat quietly in Rob's car across the street from Penn Station. It was a cold afternoon, but the streets were crowded with holiday shoppers. Barbara's hand was in mine, her bags on the back seat. She was returning to the mountains, giving me the time and space I needed to find myself. We'd write. Maybe see each other next spring. She didn't need any help with her bags. I watched her walking away and wondered about my feelings, because the sadness I felt was more than matched by a huge sense of relief. Later, I realized that she knew too much about me. I'd exposed my fears and dreams to her in those years of letters. The intimacy that held us together while I was Inside threatened me now that I was free. She reminded me of prison and parts of myself that I'd rather forget than face. I kept watching and caught a last glimpse of her long brown hair swirling in the wind, then she was gone.

23

Regards to Constantinople

Istanbul
January, 1976

Hi Billy,

Yeah, just a quick note to tell you I got the money from the Consul, along with a new guitar. Thanks, man, sometimes this guitar is all that stands between me and the Madness.

I've been transferred back into the main population. No more separate cellblock for the foreigners, I'm in with Turks and such now. No problem, after six months in isolation with those anarchist assholes, it's even good to be back with the T's.

Can't say thanks in a letter, would be too repetitious. I'm still feeling sick, as I mentioned in the last letter, but will speak more about this with pointed precision later.

Love,
Harvey

I was free, but Harvey was still inside.

I'd sent two thousand dollars of my book advance money to the American Consul in Istanbul for Harvey. It wouldn't get him out, but it would help make things easier Inside. I knew from a recent letter that he was planning to visit "Bedlam"—our slang for Section 13 for the criminally insane at the Bakirkoy Mental Hospital. We'd spent long hours talking about this before our window escape plan had failed so painfully last year. I'd told him about the madness of my Bakirkoy visit years ago when I was first arrested, and he was fascinated by the article of Turkish law that protects insane people from being held in prison.

"So, shit," he'd said, "I just convince them I'm crazy and they keep me in the hospital?"

"You don't understand," I said, "this isn't your normal hospital."

"It's gotta be easier to escape from a fucking hospital than this goddamn prison."

"And it's real hard to get a crazy report," I said, "considering all the competition."

Harvey had just laughed. "I've never had any problem convincing people I was crazy."

Now he wanted to go to Bakirkoy and get a crazy report. Getting there was really a function of bribing the prison doctor, who then recommended an observation period in the hospital. Getting a crazy report from the hospital was something else. Harvey really didn't know what he was getting into. No one could believe the madness of Bakirkoy unless they'd been there.

I had grave doubts about this plan. Even if he got to Bakirkoy and stayed there with a crazy report, escaping wasn't easy, and he'd have no help once he got over the walls. But there was a growing feeling of guilt in me, knowing he was still suffering while I was free. I began a letter-writing campaign, attempting to pressure government officials into pursuing the prisoner exchange treaty that had been in the works for years now. I didn't have much faith in this plan, but I needed to do something. Harvey's continued imprisonment was a growing cloud on my horizon.

1-5-76, Monday
Mr. Howard Mace
Consul General
Istanbul

Dear Howard,

Yes, a very happy New Year to you and everyone else over there. A new year, a fine clean new year. It feels so good to be alive and free. Events here have been moving along well. We've finished the outline of the book and are sending it off to the various publishers. Expecting some interesting replies shortly. I was out in Hollywood a few weeks ago speaking with a man about a movie. Outrageously unbelievable. But not really, I believe anything is possible in this crazy life...

And now to the important (and difficult) part of my letter. Howard, you remember your recent request to me over the phone about not mentioning Harvey's name or speaking about the 'unfortunate incident' back in Istanbul? Well, as much as I would like to honor your request, I find myself in such a position that it may not be possible. I have been in communication with him. I was there, I know how badly Harvey was beaten back in Nov. '74. I know from his letters before I escaped how the injuries he received (hernia re-opened, facial damage, etc) were troubling him. I also know that these injuries haven't been successfully treated, even up to this writing. I know that Harvey has been writing the Consul and Mr. Macomber, requesting an American Air Force doctor to help him. The responses, when they came, just didn't make it. The guy is in pain. The very air in prison is painful, but to be busted up physically at the same time is not bearable for any extended length of time. Harvey was beaten in Nov. '74. He's still hurting today. We're friends. I just can't allow this situation to continue. I must do all I can to help him.

So now we come to your request and the position I find myself in. I would like to honor your request but it seems to me that perhaps the best thing I could do for Harvey would be to use the many media contacts I've been fortunate enough to acquire, use them to help publicize Harvey's plight, perhaps start some sort of campaign to help him get the treatment needed or whatever...I don't really know what else to do. It seems all efforts on his own behalf, either with the Turkish authori-

ties or thru the Consul-Embassy have come to nothing. He needs new x-rays, proper surgery and medical opinion. He needs it NOW...

Perhaps you may have some other suggestions of what can be done to get Harvey's body fixed-up. I'd be happy to hear them. And if a way is found to help him but money is needed for doctors, medicine, etc, please inform me of the approximate amount and I'll mail it off thru Special Consular Services.

Harvey's latest letter arrived today. He's 100% in favor of the publicity approach. He's tried all other avenues without any results. He's in pain as I write this. I would very much like to hear your opinions on the situation. Hope to hear from you soon. Give my regards to Constantinople...

Thanks,
Billy

24

The Busy Bee Book Factory

During the early months of 1976, I spent my days writing about prison and my nights dreaming about it. I slept very little because I invariably woke from a nightmare, covered with sweat. Julian Bach hooked me up with a writer named Bill Hoffer, a gentle, relentless, bearded bear of a guy who helped organize and direct my efforts. The task seemed overwhelming to me. Stirring up all the memories I'd buried while in prison created havoc with my dreams. I would have quit many times if Bill hadn't kept pushing me, encouraging me to continue. I'd pump out raw verbiage which Bill would edit and clarify. I was still too close to everything and couldn't see the forest for the trees. Bill became my discerning eye and gave the project a perspective that I lacked. We worked on the book at a pressured pace from December 1975 to June 1976. We shuttled back and forth on the train between his home in Maryland and mine in New York. Our contract with E.P. Dutton had monetary penalties affixed to late delivery dates of the first, second, and final drafts. This was a "now" story, and they wanted to publish as soon as possible. We jokingly called ourselves the Busy Bee Book Factory, and with Bill's wife helping with the typing, we worked at a feverish pace because none of us wanted to lose a penny of the $25,000 advance money.

While the work was a labor of tough-love and discovery for me, it did create major difficulties. The many thoughts and images that didn't find their way onto the paper during the day often found their way into my dreams at night. The writing became a catharsis. As the book progressed and grew, as more words, events, and ideas stuck to the paper, things settled inside me. The nightmares began to fade.

25

Melissa

By night I explored the wild side of Manhattan with Marc and Melissa. She fixed me up with a series of dates, all interested in meeting the guy who escaped from Turkish prison. It was unnerving in many ways, but it got me laid a lot, and it sure beat the ugly, secret sex of prison.

Melissa and I recognized each other as playmates from our first meeting. We both loved puns and impromptu play-acting. We laughed at our own non sequiturs and found each other witty. There was an electric physical attraction between us which we kept in check because of our mutual love for Marc. Work often forced Marc out of town at the last moment, but he always insisted Melissa and I go to the parties anyway.

It was very difficult for me to understand, but one February night four months after escaping, I found myself in Melissa's apartment after a wild party where we'd danced ourselves sweaty. We were on the couch in the darkness, sipping wine, staring out at the city sparkling below us. Our legs were touching, from the knee to the ankle. Marc was out of town.

"I think I'd better leave," I said, not moving.

"Yes," she said, shifting slightly, "maybe you'd better."

I stood up.

She stayed down, staring at me.

I felt myself on the edge of an experience that wasn't within bounds. It wasn't possible. Neither of us would allow it. Then why didn't I move toward the door? Melissa raised the wine glass to her ripe, plum-colored lips. She drained it down, holding me with her eyes. She leaned forward, set the glass on the wood-slab table, and her hand brushed my thigh as she leaned back into the cushions.

"Still here?" she asked, arching back, her full, straining breasts surging against her pale silk blouse.

I couldn't move. I stood there staring down into her dark eyes. They radiated. I saw myself in a dream. I'd dreamed about her before I'd met her. She was my prison fantasy come to life. Of course it could only be a dream. Marc was my oldest friend. Melissa had lived with him the entire five years I was Inside. She knew it couldn't happen. I knew she did.

Then as her eyes moved slowly over my face and down my body, I knew it was going to happen and that the consequences would be staggering. But it didn't matter. Nothing mattered. Nothing would stop us now. Not friendship, not fear, not pain, nothing.

"Kiss me goodnight, " she said, standing, offering her cheek. I kissed her cheek. She turned her head. I kissed her mouth. She kissed back, sucking my lip. I tried to back off, but her hands encircled my ass and pulled me up close. Her hips ground into my pelvis.

"Wait!" I said, breaking away.

"Why?" she asked, pulling me in, pushing herself against me.

"What about Marc?" I asked as her hand slipped down to the bulge in my pants.

"It's over, it's been over, he doesn't care," she said, unhooking my belt.

"I don't think I can do this," I said, struggling to overcome my lust.

She stepped back and pulled her blouse up over those luscious mounds. "Do these," she said, cupping my head and pulling my mouth to a dark raspberry nipple.

One month later I was living with Melissa, and my oldest friend in the world wished I'd died in prison.

Melissa told me later that her relationship with Marc was virtually dead by the time I came home; that they were together because of inertia and economics and because it's always so hard to say goodbye. She was a funny lady—erratic, erotic, moody and unpredictable. She was a late child, her parents older, her brothers and sisters married and moved away. Her imagination had been honed by growing up alone on a small Tennessee farm. She played by herself in the fields with grasshoppers and talked to her old dog, Sam. The family was poor, the world was hard, and she'd sustained her inner joy with imagination. In her dreams she knew of far-off places and moved in different forms. Then Sam died when she was eleven, and Daddy died the following year. Her secure world shifted, and the tremors shook her for years.

She also told me about her first meeting with Marc on W. 76th Street as she was returning from a jazz dance class one bright spring day. She'd come to New York from Nashville a year before and was working at a cosmetics firm to pay the rent. She was dancing to keep her voluptuous figure, and her success could be judged by the annoying creep who'd been following her for blocks. Marc was fidgeting on the curb waiting for the light to change when Melissa approached and asked if he'd mind walking with her until the creep left. Far be it for Marc to refuse a beautiful woman in distress—especially when she's dressed in black leotards, purple suede boots and a brass-buckled snakeskin belt. They were both well-matched for the turbulent relationship that followed.

Living with Melissa was an intense experience. I'd never really lived with a woman before so had no idea how complicated it could all become. I was intoxicated by her femininity and constantly befuddled by the raging emotional interactions. I loved to watch her dress for work in the morning, see her adjust her breasts into her bra, smell the perfume she'd spray into private places, and just be privy to the intimate details of a woman's life. But the endless little adjustments and compromises—toilet seat lids, hanging up clothes, the minutiae of intimacy—were very difficult for me. I did all I could to figure her out, to educate myself about women. I read *Cosmopolitan* and *Viva* magazines, marked her period dates on my calendar, and even printed up her biorhythms in an attempt to understand the mercurial, unnerving, emotional swirlings that left me dizzy in their wake.

26

Bizarrini in the Rain

One wet spring day I went out to Marc's showroom to talk to him about the situation. He sat behind his desk, silently staring while I explained how confusing it all was to me. Marc listened while the rain beat steadily on the roof. I rambled on until there wasn't much more to say, then just sat there staring back at him, thinking of all the joys and adventures we'd shared, the halcyon days of our youth before the world had changed. He opened his desk and took out a set a car keys. "Here," he said, tossing them across to me, "why don't you see if you can get the Bizarrini out of second gear." Which, of course, would be suicide in this weather. I dropped the keys and walked out into the rain.

27

Hollywood Calling

In May of 1976, Julian called to say that a film producer named Peter Guber wanted to fly me to Hollywood to talk about a movie. This was such an outrageous concept I could hardly believe it. Six months ago I'm in prison eating beans, and now I'm sitting in First Class flying to Hollywood to discuss a movie about my prison experience? Very weird transition.

A limo picked me up at the L.A. airport and drove me to the Century Plaza Hotel. I was impressed. Of course, I was easily impressed after five years in Turkish prison.

Peter Guber was all contagious enthusiasm when we met. He pulled up in front of the hotel in a little silver Mercedes. He had a rainbow-colored lightning bolt streaking across the front of his sweater and the word FLASH emblazoned beneath it. I hopped in the car and figured this guy was going places.

I was thrilled to cruise onto the Columbia lot, past the street sets and familiar scenes I'd known from a variety of films. Peter took me to the commissary for lunch, and I gawked at the famous faces and gorgeous women while we discussed my prison experience. He took me up to an office where I told my tale to some fat cat with a cigar behind a big desk. Then, after a luscious English secretary showed me around the lot for two hours, I was back again in a larger office where two other fat cats with cigars listened to my tales of Turkish prison. I'm a great bullshitter, and Peter played me like a jukebox—"Billy, Billy, tell them about walking the wheel in the madhouse!"

We must have done well, because by the time I returned to New York there was a deal offer in Julian's office.

The terms were interesting. If I signed early, it was a big bird in the hand that would help the paperback auction. If I waited and the book was successful, it would give me greater bargaining power for the movie sale. I went for the immediate money—instant gratification. I'd receive $35,000 upon signing the contract, $90,000 when filming began, and a small percentage of the profits. I also signed away all control of the contents. If I didn't like the film, my only option was to have my name removed from the credits. It really wasn't much of an option, but then I never really expected a film to be made, anyway.

28

Harvey Goes to the Madhouse

Osman slid back the heavy metal door and Harvey stepped out into the busy stone corridor, where bright slabs of late September sunlight fell through tall, barred windows set at intervals along the dimming length.

"It's crazy today," said Osman, pocketing the package of Bafra cigarettes that Harvey slipped him. "Watch yourself out here."

Harvey nodded and moved into the flow. Inmates of diverse nationalities and with all styles of clothing moved between various cellblocks and work stations. The energy was high, bustling. It reminded Harvey of the between-class frenzy of his college days. Except that the students here at Sagmalcilar U. were majoring in different subjects.

Harvey was headed for the dispensary and the prison doctor. The severe headaches caused by the beating two years ago were becoming worse. He was having trouble focusing and was losing touch with reality. At least that's what he'd been telling Doctor Huessin before slipping him the necessary bribes.

He turned into a connecting corridor and was almost trampled by Arief the Bonebreaker and a phalanx of blue-uniformed guards.

"*Braaack!!*" shouted Arief, shoving Harvey aside and storming past. Harvey hugged the wall until they'd gone. Other prisoners quickly peeled off the walls and scurried away. Harvey knew someone was in trouble and was glad it wasn't him. Then he laughed at the irony—if a thirty-year sentence in a Turkish prison wasn't trouble, what was?

The dispensary was just a converted cellblock where individual cells were used for the bedridden, and the dining area was an all-purpose room. When Harvey arrived, several prisoners were sitting on wooden benches or pacing back and forth, cigarettes puffing behind them. Harvey nodded to a few of them and leaned back against the wall.

The office door opened, and Doctor Huessin's smiling face appeared. He had dark, protruding eyes and a Cheshire cat grin.

"Ah, my sick lambs, who is next here, where is that nurse when I need him?"

An old man with a large goiter on his neck stood up.

"Yes, Haji," said Doctor Hussein, "let us attend that love bump from Allah."

Hussein saw Harvey and his grin widened.

"And you, my strange American friend, I will see you shortly, all in Allah's good time."

Why shouldn't he smile, thought Harvey, all the bribes that slimy fucker gets. And he was about to get one more.

Which was why Harvey found himself in the back of a red prison van on a sweltering October morning, rumbling through the winding streets of Istanbul. He was headed for Bakirkoy Mental Hospital, where he was to be evaluated. He was chained to a glassy-eyed old man who muttered to himself and stared into space. Harvey twisted around and looked through the window slats—women, trees and open skies slid past his hungry eyes. He ached to be free. Arief the Bonebreaker had objected to this move, but Doctor Huessin blamed Harvey's eroding mental condition on the beatings by the guards and insisted further medical tests were needed.

Harvey was yanked away from the window slats when the old man pitched forward and spewed a stream of vomit across the van. Harvey stretched out the length of the chain, trying to avoid the rising stench. Best get used to it, he thought—Bedlam, here I come.

The van pulled up alongside the wall of the hospital. I had told Harvey about Bakirkoy—an old, sprawling complex of buildings surrounded by a great gray wall.

The back door opened and several hospital attendants in grimy white smocks reached into the van. The old man began screaming. Harvey joined in. The attendants grabbed their chains and dragged them to a small stone administrative office set in the wall. The largest attendant had white hair and a silver whistle dangling from his neck. Harvey knew from my description that this was Policebaba, who ran Section 13, where Harvey was heading.

"Lira, lira?" asked Policebaba.

The old man began his rhythmic babbling and Harvey scuttled into a corner, whimpering like he'd been struck.

Policebaba made a disgusted sound, slim pickings from these two, and ordered the attendants to search the prisoners. Harvey turned catatonic while they took his cheap watch and a few lira from his pockets.

"Lira?" asked Policebaba, examining the watch, "American dollar?" He dropped the watch in a bag with Harvey's name on it and led him into Bakirkoy.

The grounds were wild; pathways wound up and down rolling hills covered with clumps of trees and overgrown bushes. Harvey noted a huge oak tree, its branches extending out over the wall. That would be helpful, but he knew the surrounding wall wasn't the real problem.

The bushes ended and a huge gray stone wall, rough-hewn, ivy-strangled, perhaps fifteen feet high, loomed up in front of him. They approached a dark iron gate, rounded on top into an arch, nearly as high as the wall. Dull brass bolts dotted the strong iron surface. A smaller door also made of iron was set in the gate. One of the attendants twisted an old iron key into the lock, and the door swung open on squeaky hinges. Policebaba unshackled Harvey from the babbling old man and shoved them through into Section 13, the section for the criminally insane.

The door clanged shut. Sunlight beat down on a long, squat stone building set in the center of a large yard of hard-packed earth. Pale dust puffed around their shoes as they crossed to the building. They passed an old man with a gray beard who stood stone still, wrapped in a grimy sheet, staring into the sun. Several filthy, nearly naked men were squatted down in the slab of shade beside the building. One of them, an emaciated fellow with large, gleaming eyes reached out for Harvey's leg.

"Cigara? Cigara?" he asked, in a raspy voice.

Policebaba casually kicked him aside and led Harvey through the open metal door into the shaded interior. The attendants crowded Harvey and the old man into a small side room. The walls and floor were fashioned from smooth stone. Flies buzzed through the hot, oppressive air. When the attendants forced them to strip, the old man howled, but Harvey submitted docilely, hands covering his crotch. This was less out of modesty than his desire to hide the wad of money taped beneath his balls. Harvey expected to be hosed down, but the water wasn't running today, so they threw some lice powder on him, then Policebaba gave him some faded shorty pajamas and a pair of old shower sandals. While the attendants dealt with the still-screaming old man, Policebaba led Harvey out onto the ward.

It was dirty, but Harvey had seen worse. The whitewashed walls were now dark gray—cracked and moldy where they joined the ceilings in arches and curves rather than right angles. Harvey had heard this building had been a barracks for the Sultan's Janissary troops back in the 18th century. Twenty or thirty beds were neatly lined up in rows. Most had sheets and were occupied by men in clean pajamas and robes. Harvey recognized a few of them—*Kapidye* from Sagmalcilar who bribed their way here for some R&R. They smoked cigarettes, ate fruit, or read newspapers while Turkish music played on their small transistor radios. They barely glanced at Harvey.

Policebaba spread his arms and asked again, "Lira? American Consul?" indicating all this luxury could be Harvey's for a price.

It would be nice but didn't fit the plan, so Harvey just stared into the ozone. Policebaba grunted disgustedly then pushed him toward a low open archway, from which emanated a rumbling sound. Two attendants sat on a bed beside the archway, apparently guarding the passage, playing a two-card game called *Kulach*.

"American tourist," said Policebaba, pushing Harvey past them. Harvey stumbled through the archway into chaos.

A much larger room, really filthy, was crammed with one hundred or more metal-framed beds in uneven rows. He was struck by the noise level and the sense of ceaseless, jumbled movement. A large metal door was open to the sunlit yard but didn't offer much relief to the stifling air in the room.

In the near corner, just around the wall from the attendants, Policebaba showed Harvey a bed. A tall, bony man who looked like a sick spider sat hunched and naked on the filthy, urine-stained sheets. His huge, dark eyes fixed on Harvey.

"Twenty lira," said Policebaba, indicating Harvey could have this bed. Spiderman emitted an outraged shriek, but Policebaba backhanded him off the bed with one swipe of his huge arm. Spiderman tumbled to the stone floor, quickly rolled onto his feet, then hissed at Harvey through sharp, yellow-stained teeth. Policebaba raised his arm and Spiderman scuttled away. Harvey knew Policebaba was the main man to bribe around here, but he didn't want to expose his game this soon, so he just stared into space.

Policebaba took Harvey by the shoulders and pushed him down onto the bed. "Twenty lira," he said, figuring he'd collect the debt at some point. Foreign tourists had consulates to watch out for them. Harvey ignored him, into his crazy act.

Policebaba gave a disgusted grunt then rumbled back through the archway as Harvey stared out at the bizarre circus before him. The place was swarming with men fighting over sheets, blankets, beds and cigarettes. Various chants and droning singsong monotones formed a steady background hum behind shouted, emotional outbursts. Other men just sat amidst the chaos babbling to themselves—rocking, chuckling, crying. Filthy, smelly men, some stark naked, some wrapped in tattered, blackened sheets, moved around the room in meaningless, syncopated activity. Others darted around the room like sharp-eyed ferrets, looking for prey. Still others plodded in staring, blank-eyed silence.

Harvey tore the piss-stained sheet from the bunk and tossed it on the floor. Three men fought for it like starving dogs over a bone.

He turned the mattress over then curled up in a corner against the moldy, yellow wall. He fought down a burst of panic, gathered himself together. He knew it might take months to establish himself here among the damned before a chance to escape could be found. He knew he could do it. He had to.

Harvey let out a wild howl of rage and triumph, and bounded off his bed. He felt like one of the apes in *2001: A Space Odyssey.* He banged into several curious inmates and raced out the door into the sweltering yard.

The heat had forced most of the men inside. Harvey was thankful for the fresh air. He looked up at the huge wall of stone and mortar, covered on top by an old wire fence whose rusted strands and barbs were tangled and twisted beneath an overhanging weight of green dangling ivy. The mortar had fallen out in several places, leaving gaps and handholds between the stones. Harvey searched for a pattern. He was recovered enough from the beatings to make the climb, but it was very iffy. Other ways had to be found.

In the rear of the barracks, stairs led down to a basement door, bolted from the outside. A short wall about chest high jutted out from the stairwell. Harvey hopped up onto the wall and leaned against the barracks, as if to relax in the sunshine. I had told Harvey about the idea of leaping from the end of this wall toward the high wall. If you had a short length of weighted rope, you could catch it up in the barbed wire and hopefully pull yourself to the top. It looked very unlikely from where he sat.

Harvey sniffed something and turned to find a beetle nut-brown man wrapped in a filthy sheet grinning up at him and offering a smoking joint from which pungent hash fumes arose.

What the fuck, thought Harvey, when in Rome. He took a long hit off the joint and leaned back against the wall. The sun really was relaxing. Billowy white clouds rode in the blue sky above the ivy-strangled barbed wire atop the wall. A good omen, thought Harvey, like an I Ching toss—Billowy Clouds above Barbwire. Harvey knew he'd handle whatever came next.

He looked down to see Beetle Nut squatting in the basement stairwell, both hands feverishly jerking on his huge phallus.

So much for the I Ching. Harvey jumped down off the wall and continued around to the front yard, where he was surprised to find Policebaba searching for him.

"Come," said Policebaba, taking Harv's arm and steering him inside. "Doctors are here."

Jesus! Thought Harvey, how can they be here so soon? He wasn't ready for them yet. Or was he? He was stoned out of his mind, and that seemed the right place to be under these circumstances. I'd told him about the rational response syndrome—how it doesn't matter what you say in response to the doctors' questions, but rather whether you respond at all. If you're sane enough to answer the questions, how crazy can you be? I figured the best chance was to be like Scheherazade and intrigue them so they'll want to keep you there. Harvey had decided to do a Charlie Manson imitation, space-cased and creepy. If these doctors wanted weird, he'd give them weird.

29

Give It Birth and Send It Out

A relatively unknown writer named Oliver Stone came to New York in December 1976. He'd read the galleys of *Midnight Express* several times already and now wanted to speak with me before writing the screenplay. I knocked on the door of his hotel room. It swung open, and a dancing bear of a man with wild, twinkling eyes greeted me.

"Billy! Billy! Come on in, man, sit down. You want something to drink? Just buzz room service. Jesus, that was some trip you went through." Energy poured off him like sweat.

"And it's not over yet," I laughed. I liked him instantly. He was feverish with intensity. We sat in his hotel room drinking Bloody Marys and smoking joints, talking nonstop into a tape recorder ten hours a day for a week. He let me ramble on, steering and directing the flow with questions, exclamations, and short bursts of note-taking. I urged him to think aloud. I wanted to observe the workings of a screenwriter's mind. He wanted scraps, shreds, bits of information from me. He wanted nuances and shades that he'd sensed beneath the surface of the book manuscript.

Oliver gave me a script of his to read, *Platoon.* It had gotten him this writing job, but he was frustrated that no one in Hollywood would make it into a film, the Vietnam War still being too controversial. But it helped connect us as we used our respective reference points of prison and war to clarify the world of *Midnight Express* for him.

After a crazed week, Oliver said he'd be going off to some cabin in the mountains to write for a few months. I asked him how the film would compare to the finished screenplay.

"God only knows," he shrugged, "I just do my best, give it birth and send it out there."

30

Midnight Runs Over Harvey

On a dreary Monday morning in February, Harvey lay freezing beneath filthy blankets that reeked from the dampness. He was preparing for his weekly visit from the doctors. Bakirkoy was relatively quiet, most of the madmen numbed into a semblance of sanity by the cold. Except, of course, for the low, steady weeping of the filthy, rag-wrapped young man who had stabbed then dismembered his father eight years ago and had been here ever since. He lived in a state of outward stupefaction, identifying several of the older men as his father, clinging and begging their forgiveness and weeping constantly from their kicking, cursing rejection of him. His weeping crescendoed in a shrill, depth-wrenching scream, then he collapsed back against the wall, the deed burning softly in his brain.

Lovely, thought Harvey. And I'm supposed to compete with that?

Two months ago he'd given Policebaba the bulk of his money, asking that Baba take care of him until "he was better." Harvey suggested more money was available from the American Consul, as long as he remained here for treatment.

Policebaba understood.

The following week when the doctors had arrived, they found Harvey quivering in a corner, covered with excrement, a vitriolic stream of curses babbling past his chattering teeth. Policebaba dragged him into the small stone bathroom and hosed him down, explaining to the doctors that Harvey had been acting strange all week.

After that Harvey fasted for several days, then ate a hunk of hash the size of his thumb and was almost catatonic when the three doctors tried to examine him.

This week Harvey decided a little Lear might be in order. He stripped off his clothes and pushed out the door into the rainy yard, howling into the wind. Then he squatted down in a muddy corner with the cold rain beating upon him, wondering how far he had to go to convince the doctors of his madness. He knew he had some stiff competition and thought this week he'd stretch the envelope by attacking the doctors, maybe biting off one of their ears. This would surely get him classified as insane.

He'd been out in the freezing rain for an hour when he heard the phone ring inside. This usually meant the doctors were on their way. Then Policebaba appeared in the open doorway and called to Harvey. Harv was a little surprised that Baba would interrupt his preparation.

Harvey tried to ignore him, but Baba was insistent to the point of stomping across the muddy yard and dragging Harvey up by the arm.

"Sagmalcilar," said Baba, "you're going back to Sagmalcilar."

Harvey was stunned by this news and tried to twist away.

Baba grabbed his hair and wrenched him around. "You Americans write lies about us!"

Harvey had no idea what Baba was talking about but could only submit docilely when Baba threw him his clothes and the soldiers showed up in the red van, chained his wrists and drove him back to the prison.

31

A Head of Steam

In February 1977, after a whirlwind of writing and a rush by the publishers, *Midnight Express* was released. It was the beginning of an intense media campaign to promote the book, and I remember how my breath hung frozen in the pre-dawn air when I stepped from the cab in front of Rockefeller Center. The golden statue of Prometheus was covered with a thin glaze of ice, and the fire-bringer looked none too happy.

An NBC security guard checked my name off her list for the *Today Show* and instructed me to the far bank of elevators. On the 30th floor I was greeted by a pretty lady in tight black pants who suggested we go to the Green Room and take the chill off with some hot coffee. I followed her sweetly swaying ass down some empty hallways past a small room filled with video equipment, then across a quiet, high-ceilinged studio where a few technicians were testing lights and moving backdrops into place. A cameraman slid the huge bulk of his machine across the smooth stone floor in front of us, and I lightly skipped over the thick black cables slithering along behind.

The Green Room turned out to be blue, but the coffee warmed my bones and a cheese Danish settled my nerves. Other guests began arriving, and I found myself being introduced to Lillian Carter. She was quite affected when someone told her I'd spent five years in prison. She closed her eyes for a moment then opened them and looked into mine. "Yes," she said, "you've suffered a lot. But it's passed you now."

I smiled at her. "I sure hope so, ma'am."

She smiled at me. "I also have a son named Billy. You give your mama my best regards, you hear?"

"Yes, ma'am."

Jolie Gabor, Zsa Zsa's mother, overheard our conversation. "Oh, no," she said, all furs and diamonds, "such a pretty, dahlink boy like you—clean, so handsome with the shiny hair and suit—no, you couldn't be in prison all those years. No."

I looked over to see William F. Buckley giving me that smug smirk of superiority. "You, ahh, are making some money from all this promotional work, I assume?"

I was about to ask what he was promoting when Sweet Ass took me to Makeup, then led me across the back of the studio, motioning for quiet since the show had started.

She showed me a low carpeted platform off to one side, where two tall stools stood before a large backdrop of Turkey. I was on a stool having a small microphone attached to my shirtfront when Gene Shalit approached, looking hurried and distracted. With his wild shock of black hair and bushy moustache, he almost looked like a caricature of himself. I was glad it was Shalit doing the interview, because I enjoyed watching him and generally agreed with his reviews. He began attaching his own mike, ignoring the repeated questions of a prissy floor director who trailed in behind him.

"Gene? Thirty seconds, Gene. Gene? Do you hear me? Twenty-five seconds."

I could see us sitting there from two different angles on the monitors beneath the cameras. Gene turned toward me and we exchanged a quick handshake. "What's the basic story here?" he asked. "Something about prison, right? I haven't had a chance to read it yet..."

"Ten seconds, Gene," whined Priss.

"I was arrested smuggling four pounds of hashish out of Turkey, sentenced to thirty years, escaped after five."

"Thirty years?"

"Yup..."

"Five seconds, four, three..." Priss counted, then pointed a bony finger at us as the red light atop the camera flashed and we were ON, as Shalit said, "I'd like to introduce our next guest, who's written one of the most powerful and exciting stories we've read in years—Billy Hayes, author of *Midnight Special*".

32

Midnight Crashes on Istanbul

The tea in Harvey's fluted glass was cold, forgotten on the wooden table beside him. He struggled through the front page story in the newspaper. *Midnight Express* had just been published in America, and the huge wave of publicity had crashed on Istanbul. The Turkish government was outraged by charges of prison brutality and legal hypocrisy. The fact that the charges were true didn't give Harvey much satisfaction. He'd been dragged back from Bakirkoy because of this and was the only American in Sagmalcilar prison, with our national popularity definitely on the decline.

To emphasize the point, Tungei, the huge Turk who ran this cellblock, entered the dining hall with his flunkies in tow. Harvey had established a good relationship with Tungei and most of the other prisoners since being transferred here after Bakirkoy—you don't fuck with me, I won't fuck with you. He'd kept a low profile and appeared to be a sick, broken man. He also had a reputation for being slightly crazy, and this was valuable in prison.

But when Tungei spit on the headline, Harvey knew it was a bad sign.

"Your friend writes lies and disgraces our country," said Tungei, leaning across the table into Harvey's face.

"Please, join me, " said Harvey. "Would you like some tea?"

Tungei swept the glass aside and it shattered against the wall. "I don't drink with an American pig!"

Harvey stood up. "Listen, I didn't write this book, okay? And I've been here so long, I forget what America looks like."

Tungei stared while his agitated flunkies pressed forward. Harvey slowly backed away from the table. "We've always treated each other with respect, right?"

Tungei grabbed the newspaper and crumpled it in his fist. "This book makes us sound like animals. That is not respect."

"I haven't read it and I didn't write it," said Harvey, slowly reaching for the handmade blade in his back pocket. He knew it wouldn't help much, but he'd take a few of these fuckers down with him.

33

Celluloid Dreams

A hot August afternoon, six months after the book was published, I was alone in our apartment, staring out at the city spread beneath me. Melissa was at work. Harvey's most recent letters lay on my desk. He'd been dragged back from Bakirkoy because of the furor over *Midnight Express*, and conditions at Sagmalcilar were getting worse. I'd written the American Consul, the Ambassador, and various newspapers in an attempt to help Harvey, but the response was minimal.

The phone rang. It was Peter Guber, calling from L.A., speaking before the phone reached my ear.

"Billy, listen, it's all set. Everything's on. Filming begins September 12th. I want you on Malta by October 2nd. I'll be arriving the same day. Lots of press, magazines, interviews, photos, 16mm film. The works. Everything's great. Book yourself a first class ticket to Malta. Leave the return open. We may have to go to Rome or London. Bill it all to Columbia Pictures. You got all that? Any questions or problems?"

"Hi," I said, "how are you, Peter?"

Six weeks later, when Melissa and I pulled into Kennedy Airport, we were late and the place was mobbed. We'd never make the plane. I worked my way through the crowd to the ticket counter where a harried young woman was trying to deal with an irate gentleman smoking a stubby cigar. I smiled at her and lamely interrupted, "Excuse me, Miss, but our flight leaves in ten minutes and I was wondering..."

She glanced up quickly then did a double take.

"Yes, all right, sir, I'll be right with you."

I wanted to think it was due to my charm and warm smile, but I knew there were other possibilities. For the past six months I'd been on radio and TV talk shows, an endless string of morning and evening news programs, and even *What's My Line?*, as part of the book promotional tour. I was a regular mini-celebrity. It was all so weird.

For the most part it was wonderful to have people on the street tell me that after reading my book they felt like they knew me and that we were old friends. I mean, the more friends you have, the better off you are, right? But still, to be recognized by the girl at the Pan Am counter?

She finished with cigar-man then checked us through. I thanked her as she tagged our luggage. She just laughed and said, "You've flown with us before." Sure I had, but when I was arrested trying to board the Pan Am plane in 1970, it had taken me five years to make my connecting flight.

Just after takeoff the captain announced that this was Pan Am flight #110 flying to Rome, Istanbul, and Tehran. I immediately instructed a nearby stewardess to be sure to wake me in Rome if I should happen to fall asleep.

About an hour out of Rome our Alitalia jet banked through some low clouds and broke into the sunshine above the island of Malta. I was pressed against the window, staring down at the blue sea that sparkled around the tiny brown island below. It was October 2nd, exactly two years to the day since I'd escaped from the island of Imrali, and here I was landing on Malta for the filming of that event—a curious juxtaposition of realities. It really is a long way from Turkey to Hollywood.

The travel brochure told me that Malta lies at the center of the Mediterranean; it's 17 miles long, 9 miles wide, and steeped in history. As we flew in I could see the earth was dry and stony; quilt work patches of green stretched across yellow plains; low, solitary hills rose up rocky and brown.

It's an old island. On the drive to our hotel in Rabat we saw medieval battlements and walled cities topping some of the distant mesas. Gustov, our Maltese driver, took us steadily across low plains and terraced fields, and through villages of solid stone houses and narrow cobbled streets.

The Grand Hotel Verdala topped off a hill in the town of Rabat. We checked in, then stood on the balcony of our room. The view north across the island was magnificent. I scanned the far vast horizon, looking for Sicily, but saw only blue sea and sky. Closer to us the city-fortress of Mdina sat atop a nearby crest like an ancient stone crown. The massive walls flowed up out of the earth, part of the mount itself. The old stone churches above the walls lifted proud spires into the sky.

The sun was setting, and the bells of evening began sounding as we stood on the balcony. It was a lovely moment. Melissa moved against my side and I held her there, remembering a stormy evening on Imrali two years earlier and wooden boats bouncing at anchor in the harbor as darkness fell.

We had a 7:30 wake-up call Monday morning. The wooden floor was cold, so I did my yoga on the shag rug beside the bed, then stepped out onto the balcony and a clear windy October morning. I sucked in a few lungfuls of Maltese air and gazed at the sea. Again, the parallel realities—two years ago at sunrise I was running through a dream that balanced on the edge of nightmare, and now I was here to film it.

I stayed on the balcony and quietly watched the sea during breakfast. Melissa was used to my silences. My thoughts, as they often did, turned to Harvey Bell, still locked behind the walls of Sagmalcilar prison. My happiness seemed always shaded by his suffering.

Gustov arrived with the black Mercedes and drove us out to a small hotel near the set, where Mike Lehman, a nervous young

Columbia P.R. man, introduced us to the English production crew. The room was busy, bustling. There were papers piled everywhere. Notices tacked to walls. Charts and dates. Lots of beards and smiles. Vital people.

I tried to pin names on faces. I was just beginning to realize what a tremendous amount of behind-the-scenes work was involved in making a movie. We drank coffee, met more people, saw some stills, then drove out to the set with David Puttnam, the English producer. He drove an awning-topped jeep and looked a bit like Paul McCartney, circa *Abbey Road.*

His eyes lit up when I introduced him to Melissa.

"Are you an actress?" he asked, looking at her cleavage.

"Sometimes," she said coyly, smiling at him.

The set was impressive—Fort St. Elmo, an old stone fortress, heavy and foreboding, perched on cliffs above the sea. The Knights of Malta had held out gallantly here against Turkish invaders during the Great Siege of 1565; now the crew had turned it into a Turkish prison.

A cobblestone road passed through a narrow rock archway then sloped down into the dusty "prison" courtyard. Three tiers of balcony ramps lined the outside of the prison across from the road. Alan Parker was down in the yard with the camera crew, directing a scene up on the second balcony. The three principal actors, Brad Davis, Randy Quaid, and John Hurt, were leaning out over the rusty iron railing, arguing about something. Sound was rolling. Grips held mikes out on long poles.

We stopped halfway down the ramp and watched the scene through barbed wire. We were level with the second balcony, looking right at the actors, forty yards away.

It was extraordinary for me.

I tried not to stare at Brad. I'd seen him before on TV. I knew who he was. Or did I? I mean, he was me! I looked in at the prison through the barbed wire and saw myself staring out.

Brad was brooding and intense, listening to Randy argue about escape. It was a foolish plan and Brad knew it. Still, Randy was affecting him.

"Listen, man," said Randy in a fierce whisper, "I don't know about you guys, but if I don't get out of here soon, ah'm not gonna make it!"

I thought of Harvey and his mad intensity.

I saw the strain of decision on Brad's face. There was a knot in my own stomach.

A plastic cup clattered on the stones off to the right.

"Cut!" shouted Alan. "Stop the bloody noise!"

"Quiet!" screamed an assistant with a bullhorn, yelling at the Maltese extras smoking and drinking coffee against the wall. "You blokes are being paid to do nothing today, so sit still and be quiet and do bloody nothing, or I'll send you all home!"

David called down to Alan, who saw us and smiled. His long brown hair, baggy pants and loose shirt reminded me of some Impressionist painter. Which, in a way, is what he was.

He shook my hand with a big open smile. "Hello, Billy, been wanting to meet you for a while now. Look around, I'll be with you in a bit."

We followed David down into the yard. The place felt so real it staggered me. I was there again. I was back. A raggedy bunch of

"Turkish" kids were huddled beside the gate as we entered. I responded instantly. "*Merhaba*," was on my lips before I realized they were Maltese children hired as extras. But their costumes were perfect, their faces dirty, and their eyes held that same look of worldliness that street kids everywhere seem to have.

I turned away with a laugh, then froze.

Two Turkish cops were standing ten feet in front of me. I was stunned; adrenalin pumped through my body. It took an instant to realize that, again, they were just extras. I turned back and almost bumped into a huge hulking man in a Turkish prison guard uniform. He scowled at me, and although one part of my mind knew this was Paul Smith, the actor, another part responded to Hamidou, my prison nemesis. Then his face creased in a big smile and his extended paw enveloped my hand.

"Billy," he whispered, "really great to meet you. Whew, some story."

"Quiet on the set!" yelled the Assistant Director.

Paul and I turned to watch the scene being shot, and I reached out for Melissa's hand.

Later David led us into a dark doorway and up a set of stone stairs to my bunk. Faded photos were taped to the grimy walls; Turkish graffiti scrawled on the stone—it felt very real. A torn picture of my girlfriend was taped up there next to some pornography ripped from a Turkish magazine. I whacked the coarse brown blanket of my bed, and dust rose in a soft cloud. I stretched out and stared up at the rusty springs of the bunk above.

No one spoke.

I closed my eyes and began to drift; I knew it was only a movie set, but could feel myself sliding out of the moment. It was exciting and terrifying to think I might really be back in prison again, waking from a dream when I opened my eyes. The fear was so close I could taste it.

I balanced there for a moment, then a voice was speaking somewhere, far off. I focused on it and pulled myself back. The lumpy bedsprings were digging into my back. David was asking, "Billy, what do you think? Billy?"

"Ah, yes." I opened my eyes to the movie set, not the prison. "Yes, you've got the flavor of the place, all right." I rolled over for a look under the bunk. Empty. "But you need some stuff under the bunk."

"Stuff?"

"Yeah, boxes, rags, odds and ends. You never throw anything away in jail. Store it all up under your bunk. The guards throw everything out periodically during searches, but it just accumulates again. Need lots of stuff and junk under the bunk."

David made a mental note of this. I felt helpful.

"Want to see the room where the beating took place?" he asked.

I wasn't so sure but went along anyway.

It was a cold stone cubicle with a barred window in the ceiling and one narrow doorway.

"The ropes were tied to those," said David, indicating two old metal rings high up on the wall. "We shot the beating last week. Really quite a powerful scene."

I'm sure.

"Come along, I'll show you."

A white stucco room at the top of the fort was being used as the cutting room. The film and a separate audio tape were hand-fed into a small viewer. I reminded myself to be objective and watch these rushes with a critical eye, but the film had barely flickered onto the screen before I was sucked in and caught between the images in front of me and the memories behind me. It lasted about five minutes, until the film flickered out and flapped around the reel a few times. The room was silent. I blinked. I was sweating. Some objective observer.

I laughed to relieve the pressure. "Whew! Powerful."

David nodded. "Right."

I forced a smile and made a gesture with my hands to indicate enough rushes for today. I stepped outside and took a deep breath of fresh air. A pair of arms slipped around my waist. Melissa always knew when I needed a hug.

I spent several hours wandering around the set while a 16mm crew filmed my reactions for the publicity campaign. Then at lunch I met John Hurt, the English actor who was playing Max, a lovable but sickly junkie friend of mine. The physical resemblance between John and Max was startling. He had the clothes and mannerisms, and had shaved portions of his head to give himself a balding, stringy-haired look. But the resemblance went further. Max was shooting a codeine-based medicine that affected his eyes and stomach. John was so intently into the part that he'd somehow developed stomach problems and had a small cyst forming on his right eyelid.

"My God," he laughed, "this part is really beginning to get to me."

Two days passed and I still hadn't met Brad. David Puttnam said Brad was so intently into his part that he was reluctant to meet me. He was Billy Hayes, in prison twenty-four hours a day and didn't want to come out of character. It might be hard for him to hold the reality he'd created for himself if confronted by this strange prison person in the flesh. I understood but was disappointed. I wanted to meet the guy who was playing me.

Late that afternoon David led me back up the stone steps in the back of the fort. He said they'd dressed the floor under my bunk and wanted my opinion on it. We turned a corner into the room, and there was Brad sitting on the bunk, the lights burning and the cameras rolling. Brad looked up, surprised to see me. I pulled back but David urged me forward.

"Go on," said David, "if I've got to do this, I'm bloody well going to get it on film."

I hesitated, then slowly walked towards Brad.

"Oh, man, this isn't fair," Brad said, obviously unaware that the meeting had been arranged.

I sat on the bunk opposite him, our knees almost touching. "I know, it's a surprise for me, too."

We stared at each other, some unique bond immediately apparent. Then a huge grin crossed Brad's face and he held out his hand.

"Fuck it," he said, "I'm really glad to meet you."

I shook his hand hard. "Yeah, me too."

34

Escape to California

Melissa and I were arguing a lot by the time we got back to New York. I was confused about who I was and what I wanted. I'd discovered how demanding a relationship could be, and how much honesty and self-evaluation were involved.

It didn't help that the Turkish government was upset with the book and that there were protests and media denunciations of me and my story in both Turkey and America. I was stopped by strangers on the street who knew intimate details of my life. Even though the personal response I got from people was overwhelmingly positive, it was still difficult for me to accept. I felt exposed and confused. I was becoming paranoid, afraid Turkish agents might jump out from behind a door, chloroform me and drag me back to Turkey. I bought a small 6-shot derringer and started carrying it everywhere. Though my phone number was unlisted, there were still ugly, late night phone calls—even to my parents' house. This really bothered me. I'd caused them all that pain while I was Inside, now they were still being punished for what I'd done.

I lay in bed one winter morning watching Melissa hurry into her clothes, late for an appointment with her shrink, Eddie. She checked her tape recorder and pulled a cassette from her desk drawer. The phone rang and she picked it up.

"Thanks, Carl, I'll be right down." Her cab was waiting.

I heard her open the drawer in the hall where she kept her diaphragm.

"See you tonight, Baby," she yelled, her heels clicking out the door.

"Bye, Babe," I called, looking across at the cassette tape she'd left on the desk. I threw back the covers and padded into the hall. The diaphragm was gone. I crossed to the windows. New York's panorama spread before me—defiant stone beneath a cold gray sky. I looked down at the top of a yellow cab idling in the wet black street below and saw Melissa rush from the building. As the cab sped away, I lifted the cassette from her desk and popped it into my tape recorder.

Melissa and I took a trip to Peru. We fought all the time, then made up with passionate bouts of sexual fury. We made desperate love in a fog-shrouded ruin high atop Machu Picchu, then descended into the thick Amazon jungle beyond Quito where we were surrounded by black iridescent butterflies, lazy alligators, and insects the size of birds that crashed into the mosquito netting around our hammock.

There in the rainforest I confronted her about sleeping with Eddie, not mentioning I'd listened to the tape of their sessions. She denied it at first, but I pressed her and she broke down in tears, saying she needed Eddie, that he was like a father to her and she'd been fucking him for years. That it didn't mean anything.

I knew from the tape that she thought I was a dreamer and that she couldn't rely on me. I knew she loved our passion, but she was afraid I was too irresponsible to take care of her. She had a deep need for a strong man to protect her from the cold hard world. I knew she was with me until I grew up or she found that man. I was hurt by her doubts and shaken by their validity.

We had a final scene in the jungle with much crying and bitterness. We returned upriver to Lima where I grabbed the next plane to New York. I loaded my possessions into the new Volvo I'd bought with the first advance movie money, strapped my bicycle to the roof, and headed for California. I thought it would be a new place where no one knew me, where I could re-discover myself and start fresh.

35

Give Me the Fucking Dime

February, 1978: It was freezing in New York, and a balmy 81 degrees in Los Angeles. I went from 34th Street in Manhattan to 42nd Street in Manhattan Beach, from twenty-one floors above the city to a sloping hillside above a sandy beach and an eye-stretching ocean. My newly purchased surfboard was on the balcony of my small apartment. I lay on the rug, jazz on the radio, realizing I was finally living alone. Since escaping I'd lived with my folks, my brother, and then Melissa. Now I was alone. I nestled down into the feeling; this was what I thought I needed. Now what do I do with it?

What I liked most about the all the publicity work I'd done was the energy that passed back and forth with a live audience. A month before the Amazon trip I'd decided to take some acting classes, and had wandered into a class at H.B. Studio in Greenwich Village. I loved it, and determined to pursue acting when I moved to Los Angeles.

Though I'd changed geography, I still had the same old fears and uncertainties. When I meet Eric Morris, a highly respected, completely mad acting teacher, he instantly connected with me and saw through all my shields and masks. He became my teacher and friend.

Eric's work demanded emotional honesty. It forced me to confront, accept, and eventually to utilize all the myriad parts of myself. This process of self-discovery was terrifying—I began taking three classes a week. It became my therapy.

I hold my outstretched palm in front of each class member as I slowly work my way around the circle, an exercise designed to express your need. "Give me the dime. I need the dime. Could I please have a dime? I really need it."

"Do you?" asked Eric.

"Yes."

"How bad is your need? Nobody's responding to you, are they?"

"No."

"Nobody gave you the dime, right?"

"Right." I was getting a little tired of this shit.

"So, either you don't really need it, or you're not willing or not able to express your need."

Silence.

"How bad is your need? It all just sounds like bullshit and words to me."

"So what the fuck do you want?"

He leapt to his feet shouting. "I want you to show us how much you fucking need! How much you hurt! How much you needed in prison but could never express or accept or even cry about because you thought it made you look weak. You still do!"

"What do you know about it!" My chest felt like it was imploding. I stalked out of the circle. "I don't need your fucking dime!"

"You need it like air," Eric shouted at my back. "And we're dying to give it to you, but you've got to open out to let us in..."

36

Helping Harvey?

No matter how far I ran, I kept confronting myself. I couldn't forget about Harvey, still sitting in prison while I rode my bike along the beach in California. I sent him money and wrote continual letters to public officials attempting to implement the Prisoner Exchange Treaty, but I really didn't believe it was going to free him. And neither did he. We'd both heard it all too many times before and knew that if you really want something done, you have to do it yourself. But what could I do? Go back to Turkey and break him out? This bizarre scenario was slowly beginning to appear like the only solution. I'd been advising Harvey to sit tight and wait, but that's so hard to do when the days of your life are slipping away and each morning you wake to find yourself still behind bars. Harvey came up with a variety of escape plans, but I didn't have confidence in them; I wanted to help him escape, but certainly didn't want him to get killed trying.

April 4, 1978

Hi Billy,
    My head's leveled off enough to write you a straight letter. I'm pissed off at you because you, of all people, have no right to play Big Daddy and tell me to sit tight and wait for a Prisoner Exchange treaty that you didn't sit tight and wait for...

And yeah, I've caught an incredible amount of bullshit from the Turks because of Midnight Express and you've been out there making money and apparently thinking of nothing but making money (that's how it looks from here) and it galled me for you to lay that 'stay put' crap on me. It would piss you off if the situation were reversed.

I'm wasting more stamps to tell you this because, oddly enough, I want to stay friends and I'm straight out telling you what's bothering me.

One thing that's currently bothering me is the Turk heroin smuggler who used the plan I outlined to you (because you asked me to) last summer and escaped from the Madhouse last week...The truth is I think you're afraid someone else will cut in on your act, Billy. Jealousy. Fuck that. I don't care about writing a book, particularly a book you've already done. So what's up?

Billy, fuck money. I'm sorry now I ever accepted a penny from you. If I had the money I'd give it back to you. Fuck! Obviously we've both changed a lot. The thought that you think you can throw money at me and I'll be a good monkey is the ultimate insult to my last remaining shreds of integrity.

Look, I'll spell it out. You talked big but you didn't come through. That's the scene in a nutshell. And I didn't expect that from you...Good luck anyway and take care of yourself.

Harvey

It was becoming increasingly more difficult to evaluate my obligation to Harvey. He kept writing with outlandish scenarios for escape, all of which seemed to be suicidal from where I read them in California. But I knew how different the perspective was when you were behind bars in Istanbul.

Willie,

I just got back my umphteenth request to open prison – refused –! I talked to Lynet, the mudir. He called Ankara. They said it's because of what you did. Fact. So one and a half years ago I could have been in an open prison. Yes. And Robert. And the girls.

Well, fuck this pride shit, willie. You asked if I needed money. Of <u>course</u>! why should I sit here unstoned and ~~miserable~~ when I'm stuck here for the very reason you're stoned and comfortable?

Its a very wierd situation, but if you think I'm bullshitting, write the General Prison Director – or ~~just~~ write Camul Higgins, Richard, Istabul. It twists my head whenever someone puts it into words as the good mudir did. Willie, it's not just me. <u>No</u> tourist can go to an half open or open prison. Because of "M.E."

And am I blaming you? Fuck, I don't know. I'm not in a position to know all that came down. I remember writting you in 1975 and saying – "Sock it to 'em, willie. Tell 'em this and that." So I'm just as guilty as you. Anyway – that's what's been driving me up the wall – this wall I can't get beyond – Sagmalcilar.

37

The Lemon Theory

One of my literary agents in New York suggested I meet with a client of hers in Los Angeles, Don Chastain, if I was really interested in acting. She said he was an actor, writer, and jazz singer extraordinare who knew the ropes, and that we'd hit it off. My white Volvo was still grimy with cross-country dirt when I followed Don's phone directions up a winding Mulholland Drive—still amazed by the exotic flora and fauna of California—to an old, rambling, castle-like house in the Hollywood Hills. Don's apartment was a small wing of the house, nestled into the side of the ivy and cactus covered slope, looking out across the San Fernando Valley at the San Gabriel Mountains in the distance. A weathered redwood door opened onto a big strapping Marlboro Man with a smile as wide as the Oklahoma sky where he was raised. He grabbed my outstretched hand, "Whew, man, that's some kinda trip you been through, c'mon in, glad you made it."

Energy poured off him. The walls were covered with posters of Broadway shows he'd been in, including a road tour of *Applause,* where he was Lauren Bacall's leading man. "Wow, traveling with Lauren Bacall," I blurted, "*that* must've been something." That huge grin lit up his handsome face again, then he motioned toward a massive, rough-hewn coffee table where a white joint lay at the center of a marble chess set. We lit the joint, settled into the game, and had instant simpatico. Don was a few years older than me, and became a mentor and guide through the jungle of Hollywood. Our synchronicity continued when *Midnight Express* was chosen for the upcoming Cannes Film Festival, where a film Don had written, *The Mafu Cage,* was also being shown. Don mentioned that I should meet his young cousin, Wendy, who'd been traveling in Europe and was helping them out at the festival.

"You'll like her," said Don, "she's cute and blonde and has a nice ass."

May, 1978: I found myself sipping champagne in the first class section of a TWA jet bound for France. I was excited and my mouth was dry. The plane was full of Hollywood celebrities—David Soul raucously drunk across the aisle; Jackie Bisset lounging beneath huge sunglasses two rows ahead; Brooke Shields looking indecently young and delicious. *Midnight Express* was entered in the Cannes Film Festival, and success there translated into big box office, so competition among major studios to woo the critics and influence the media was intense.

Columbia Pictures had decided it would be a great idea to have the "real" Billy Hayes on hand to speak with the press and add a stamp of authenticity to the film. I'd been dating Cathy, an English secretary who worked for Peter Guber, and learned from her that several studio executives were slightly nervous about using me to promote the film. They already felt that Brad Davis was a loose cannon, and she said they considered me to be something of an opportunist, which, coming from them, I took as a compliment. They wanted me highly visible, creating interest in the movie through media appearances, but they were concerned with my acting aspirations. They said I wasn't haggard enough to fit their image of an escaped con. Many felt I was already too articulate ("slick," some called it) and felt it would hurt my credibility, and thereby the movie's, if people knew I was studying to be an actor. "An actor learns to lie," they said, "and people may doubt what he's saying." I'd been discovering from Eric just the opposite—that an actor must learn to be open and honest—but their attitude towards acting said a lot in itself.

In my brief but dizzying dealings with the movie industry, I'd tried to balance between being too cynical and too naive, although Don said you can't be too cynical. Whatever, it was a pragmatic business, and I was basically a pragmatist—they use you, you use them. Brad Davis called it the Lemon Theory—as long as they can squeeze juice out of you to promote their film, then it's limos and luxury. When the juice is gone, they toss the rind on the garbage heap and look for the next lemon. The trick, of course, is to stay juicy.

Shit, I didn't mind. I'd been running on the beach for three months and was tanned and healthy—I felt vital and full of juice. I did think there might be opportunities to advance my fledgling acting career. I was scared of all the upcoming attention, but you can't let your fear stop you. I'm sipping champagne on my way to Europe to see the movie version of my experience—how bad can that be?

Cannes is a typical little resort town on the French Riviera—quaint and quiet in winter, buzzing with suntanned tourists in summer. For two weeks each spring Cannes hosts the Film Festival and the town goes wild, caught up in the mad, swirling magic of the movies. The elegant white beachfront hotels fill to capacity with producers, directors, and international stars whose reservations have been made months, even years, in advance. The Festival is a gaudy media carnival and a hard-nosed marketplace. Scores of small independent filmmakers come to exhibit their works, hoping to attract one of the major studios to finance the risky and expensive distribution of their movies. Dazzling jet-set parties and opening night premieres mark the major films in competition for the top prizes and the prestigious Palme D'Or award. Willowy young starlets, desperate to be discovered, stalk hotel lobbies and restaurants; traffic moves at an escargot's pace along the famous Croisette, the palm-lined waterfront street jammed with excited fans and frenzied photographers; shrewd lawyers-turned-producers make million-dollar deals over lunch on the tiled terrace of the Carlton Hotel.

I was tired but excited when we finally landed in Nice. On the winding coast road to Cannes, I watched the brilliant afternoon sun sparkle off the blue Mediterranean and listened as Michael, Columbia's nervous young P.R. man, brought me up to date on developments. He was wired and agitated, as usual.

"Puttnam and Parker are already here," said Michael, scratching his nose, "staying at the Carlton with you. Peter Guber's up the coast, of course, at Cap d'Antibes. Brad Davis is due in soon. I picked up your girlfriend, Melissa, this morning and booked her into your suite."

My decision to bring Melissa to Cannes was a balance of guilt and lust. We'd spoken a few times since I left New York, and she'd reminded me of my earlier promise to take her. She desperately wanted to go and whispered some sweet scenarios about what was always the best part of our relationship. I relented, but was regretting it now.

"We're all gathering for an informal dinner tonight," said Michael, looking at his notes, "to discuss tomorrow's schedule. In the afternoon we've got an extremely important press conference." He looked over at me. "You and Brad need to be on your best behavior." Michael didn't think Brad or I took this seriously enough. "The black-tie premiere is later that evening. You remembered your tux, right?"

"Yeah, the white suit I told you about." It was a John Travolta disco number that Melissa bought me because it was tight on my ass. Why waste money renting a tux?

"You guys should get to bed early tonight and be well rested. It's gonna be hectic the next coupla days."

The strain of the job was apparent on Michael's pale, thin face.

"Shit, you're the one needs the rest," I said. "And get out in the sun, Mikey, you're way too pale."

He just laughed and went on jabbering about schedules and such. Six months later he'd be found dead in a tub, his wrists slit and his young life draining out onto the bathroom floor.

The Carlton Hotel was the throbbing heart of the Festival. At the porticoed entrance a pack of aggressive photographers and curious onlookers kept a steady vigil, eager for a glance of the rich and famous as they arrived in Ferraris, Mercedes, and chauffeured limousines.

When we arrived the elegant lobby was buzzing with activity, thronged with guests and press. Movie posters and stenciled notices were taped to marble columns. A makeshift marketplace of small booths was set up against the gilded walls, with stacked boxes sitting beneath folding tables piled with pamphlets and information about the myriad films and activities available.

I glanced into the smoky bar where white-vested waiters scurried among crowded tables. The air rang with laughter and animated conversation. The immediate impression was one of wealth and power—expensive clothes, thin gold watches, sleek, suntanned women and hard-eyed men. I saw Francis Ford Coppola sitting in a corner behind his black beard and thick glasses. Rumor had it he'd spent 40 million dollars on *Apocalypse Now*, including every penny of his personal fortune. I'd kill to work for him.

Brooke Shields and Keith Carradine wandered in from the terrace, followed by a line of baggage handlers and a string of reporters.

I followed a porter down a carpeted hallway, and when we turned a corner Melissa was suddenly striding towards me—brown hair piled high atop her head and a red jumpsuit clinging to her delicious curves. She rushed into my arms, and our bodies fitted together like two halves of a broken mold.

In the room we tore off our clothes and made frenzied love. Then we lay quietly in each other's arms. She was crying softly. I was feeling guilty. She had so much love to give but needed so much strength and support in return. I was afraid of responsibility and barely felt capable of taking care of myself.

I held her close and said nothing as the light faded from the sky.

I was up with the sunrise, running along the seawall beside the quiet harbor. I followed the railroad tracks out beyond the sleepy town. I needed to run to balance the energy, to keep me grounded. The glassy sea reflected the glorious colors of the dawn, and the opalescent air filled with birdsong. I thanked The Sky for the moment.

On my way back into town I came upon two wheezened Frenchmen slowly strolling beside the water—old friends sharing the simple magic of the morning. I thought about Harvey.

Brad and I had a series of interviews and photo sessions scheduled on the Carlton Terrace later that morning. I stopped by his room and we got stoned before coming downstairs, the better to deal with our ambivalence about interviews and being the center of attention. We thrived on it and at the same time were threatened by it.

Brad was thoroughly confident of himself as an actor but mildly terrified of interviews. He really cared about *Midnight Express* and knew it had already generated a great deal of controversy. He also knew some of the interviewers might be less than objective.

"Suppose," he said, taking a hit off the joint, "they ask me about drugs and stuff. Or if I've ever been in jail? What could I say that wouldn't have them scribbling in their notebooks and underlining shit?" He was worried about hurting the film, exposing one of the less-polished facets of his sparklingly, bizarre personality and having it turned into *National Enquirer* headlines.

"Fuck it," I said, taking the joint, "tell them the truth."

"What about sex?"

"What about it?"

"Suppose they ask about...Sam?"

"Oh, well, wait a minute," I said. Sam was Brad's horny old husky dog who humped everything that moved unless Brad relieved him of the strain occasionally. "*National Enquirer* just might find a story in Brad Davis beating off his dog."

"So you think maybe I shouldn't talk about that," said Brad, fixing his dark shades.

"Guber and Puttnam would probably be happier if you slid around that story."

We both laughed and decided to snap bow ties onto our t-shirts and jeans ensembles.

Michael was waiting when we strolled down the wide curving staircase that led to the lobby. "Cute," he said, looking at our outfits. "Now if you two are sufficiently prepared...we'll join the others and meet the press."

Michael led us out onto the terrace. It was only 11:00 a.m., but all the tables were full and the energy level was high. Brad winced as bright sunlight struck his sensitive, bloodshot eyes. He was a creature of the night, not usually up this early, and had irritated his eyes even more by trying to insert a pair of bright green contact lenses.

He grabbed a passing waiter and ordered a double Courvoisier on the rocks for himself and a double orange juice for me. We locked arms and strolled toward the waiting group around the Columbia table.

Peter Guber, David Puttnam and Alan Parker were already there, being interviewed by several journalists who played musical chairs between them. As director, Alan received the brunt of the adverse questioning, having to defend the film against charges of racism, homophobia, and distortion. Brad and I mugged it up for the photographers, who seemed delighted by our contrasting looks and matching bow ties. We got separated and when I next looked up, Brad was posed against a 20-foot high photo of himself on the billboard behind us. We made eye contact and burst out laughing.

During the interviews Brad ordered five plates of caviar and three bottles of champagne, offering some to all the journalists who crowded around him. I could see Michael nervously totaling up this massive lunch bill. Brad winked at me and laughed.

When I looked up, Melissa was crossing the Croisette in her tiny red bikini, heading for the beach. I knew she'd be topless the moment she hit the sand. She waved and couldn't resist a quick pouting pose. I waved back, but now that my lust was appeased, my guilt was rising. I really didn't want her here but didn't want to hurt her anymore. I felt like a shit.

I needed an afternoon run before the big premiere that evening. I sprinted through the lobby of the Carlton in my shorts and running shoes and dashed across the Croisette toward a huge crowd circling an old black Citroen parked beneath a towering palm tree. Edy Williams, the perennial American porno star, was stripping atop the car, while a howling mob of photographers and onlookers screamed at her.

At the edge of the crowd I noticed a birdlike old Frenchwoman dressed in black, shaking a cane in the air. She was screaming for everyone to move away so she could get to her car. Edy shook her tits, the crowd roared and no one even noticed the old woman. I thought it was a great metaphor for the Festival.

And then, that night at the premiere, at the height of the madness, Don's luscious little cousin from Oklahoma, Wendy Lee West, a twenty-three year old, 5'2" blonde with wide, blue-green eyes and a calm certainty about her, led me out onto the dance floor and changed my life. I didn't know it at the time. It wasn't an instant change. When the music ended Melissa reclaimed me, the bubble burst, and the crowd swallowed up the blonde angel.

Then Phillip Niarchos introduced himself and invited me out to the family yacht, the *Atlantis*, anchored like a dream in the harbor.

I turned when one of the chanting Turkish protestors outside the Palais suddenly rushed the doors and was restrained by attendants. "This movie is a racist lie!" he screamed, above the pounding disco beat of the orchestra.

I turned around and a dark-eyed woman thrust a microphone into my face. "You don't treat Turkish people very well in this movie," she said.

"They didn't treat me very well," I snapped, grabbing Melissa's hand and heading for an exit.

"You hate the Turks, then?" asked the woman, following me.

I stopped. "No. I don't hate the Turks. But the prison is brutal, the legal system sucks and I've got friends who are still in there."

I pushed open a side door and led Melissa out into the thick, surrounding darkness. The night was lit by a huge full moon that left deep shadows beneath the towering palms. We rushed into a dark pool and I pressed her against a thick smooth trunk. She clawed at my white pants and I tore the lace panties off her. We made furious love against the tree with the sounds of the celebration tinkling in the background.

She was crying as we finished. "Don't leave me, Billy, don't leave me."

"Shhh, it will be all right," I said, knowing this was the last time we'd be together.

I didn't sleep much that night. My morning run, later than usual, was constantly interrupted by people who recognized me from the newspapers and interviews. I was mobbed in the lobby of the hotel, but David Puttnam quickly detached me from the reporters and took me aside. He was furious.

"Have you seen this!" He held a newspaper with a topless photo of Melissa, strutting her shapely stuff for the cameras.

"She looks great," I said.

"She doesn't look great, she looks fucking terrible," said David, whacking the paper with his hand. "It's bad enough you looked like a bloody white knight in that suit last night—"

"The fuck you talking about?" I asked.

"—but now your girlfriend is flashing her tits for the press and telling them how she plans to become an actress."

"So what?"

"So, we're having enough credibility problems with this film already without you two looking like cheap publicity artists."

"Jesus, David, relax. And Michael told me the white suit was fine."

"Michael's a bloody idiot. Don't you realize how this could jeopardize the film? A lot of people would like to discredit our movie. Is that what you want?"

"Of course not," I said, confused by these events.

"Then you've got to be aware of what you're doing. You and Brad are under the microscope here. If you fuck up, it hurts the movie."

I didn't want that to happen.

"All right," I said. "I'll be careful and talk to Melissa."

"Get her out of town, I'm warning you, or she could blow this whole thing out of the water."

"Aren't you overreacting?"

"This kind of shit can wreck the film," he said, handing me a plane ticket. "There's a noon flight to Paris. We've reserved a room for her at the George V. Tell her you'll meet her in a couple of days, and we'll try to weather the storm."

I'd had my doubts about David after the setup he'd arranged for my first meeting with Brad, but I could feel the storm of controversy *Midnight Express* was stirring up. It felt bad, but I agreed to get Melissa out of town.

She fumed as the taxi screeched toward the airport. Amid tears and shouts she'd thrown her clothes into her suitcase and we'd slipped out the back of the Carlton. Now we rode in thick silence while guilt rose like bile in my throat. Melissa said Puttnam was getting revenge because she'd rejected his advances at the premiere the night before. She stayed stoic right up to the gate, then turned and clung to me.

"Oh, Billy, don't let them run me out like this, please!"

"I'll see you in two days," I said, lamely, as she turned and ran toward the plane.

I heard her crying in my head all the way back to the Carlton. I tried to cross the lobby but was recognized and quickly surrounded by a crowd of reporters and onlookers.

"Eh, it's the real one. Midnight Express, over here, over here!" Questions flew, cameras flashed and hands reached out to pat my shoulder. I tried to get away but couldn't.

A dark-haired man was pumping my hand, saying, "You're a hero, Billy, people can learn from your courage." I broke away and bolted up the wide carpeted stairs while the man shouted, "A hero...a real hero..."

38

Oklahoma Lady

Back in California, Wendy and I began a serious relationship, and it was immediately apparent to me that beneath the lusty exuberance, we also shared a much deeper bond. It was so strong it scared me. I feared commitment and stubbornly held on to my emotional isolation, but Wendy was even more stubborn. She was a fifth generation Okie; her grandparents' land homesteaded in the Land Run of 1889. Her strength and stability both attracted and frightened me. She told me straight out what she wanted-marriage, a loving relationship and a family. She knew I was afraid to commit and said she'd give me some time. But that if I couldn't get up the balls to do what we both knew was the right thing, then she'd walk and not turn back. And I knew this woman meant every word she said.

39

Harvey's Dilemma

October 2, 1978

Willie,
...Elia Kazan, the director of On the Waterfront *came to Turkey and bad rapped* Midnight Express. *The Turks tried to get him to make a prison film but he wisely refused. They dredged up Yilmaz Guney—a Turk film star serving a murder sentence for shooting a Turkish judge who had previously sentenced him to prison—and he says things like, "It's easy to escape from prison but we don't because we are gentlemen." Old Yilmaz got a vacation from prison for copping out, plus European exposure and probably money as well. Prison is depicted as a clean place where everyone sits around dressed in fashionable clothes drinking tea and conversing on high intellectual planes. Yilmaz is in one of the other prisons in Turkey. I don't think he could get by with that shit in Sagmalcilar.*
Billy, they won't give any foreigner a transfer now because of the M.E. publicity. I've written the Turk General Mudir, The U.S. Civil Rights Bureau, President Carter, The Civil Liberties Union, The A.C.L.U., Ambassador, etc. I can't get out of Sagmalcilar. So that's why I've been "quiet." I had a crazy chat with the 2nd Mudir... He was visiting and when someone said I was an American he started bad rapping M.E. I told him that in essence M.E. was true, that all fictionalized

Willie,

I meant to collect all the "fotoroman" installments of midnight Express which the newspaper "Günaydin" was running but they stopped it without a word on the fifth installment. Last frame I saw you were being led off to the nuthouse again. Elia Kazan, the director who did "On the Waterfront" and writes novels, came to Turkey and badrapped M.E. The Turks tried to get him to make a prison film but he wisely refused. A few weeks later they imported a lady Swedish T.V. documentary filmmaker and the Turks set to work making their counter-M.E. propaganda film. They dredged up Yilmaz Güney - a Turk film star serving a murder sentence for shooting a Turkish judge who had previously sentenced him to prison - and he says things like "It's easy for us to escape but we don't because we are gentlemen" Old Yilmaz get a vacation from prison for copping out, plus European exposure and probably money as well. Prison is depicted as a clean place where everyone sits around dressed in fashionable clothes drinking tea and conversing on high intellectual plains. Yilmaz is in Toptashi or Pashakapi Cezaevi - one of the 2 other slams in Istanbul. I don't think he could get by with that shit in Sagmalilar, *events were drawn from actual events: murders, homosexuality, dope, informers and administrative corruption were things I had personally witnessed. He couldn't answer that so he started cussing America, the Embassy, Carter, you. Finally I said, "Look, you can curse everyone you want but if you include my family when you curse, I'll have to punch you in the nose." There were a lot of Turk prisoners around us and everybody shut up. So did the 2nd Mudir. The foregoing story depicts how things have changed around here. The prison administration is scared. They have a prison scandal on their hands. I've seen— been in—half a dozen major riots.*

...The Communists started digging a tunnel six months ago—against my advice. It was busted four months later. To make the Communists look stupid the "Fascists" (Turk Nationalists-Expansionists) staged a mass escape in broad daylight. Thirteen men escaped through a visiting cabin by cutting the steel bars at the top. Of course, they'd bribed a guard...

...So I spent the money you sent on a nice new suit. I talked to the fascists about the best way out for me. They say the Madhouse. Toss a gun over the wall at a pre-arranged time in broad daylight. Wait till night if necessary and walk out. There's an organization Outside who will deliver the gun. Also, they're honest. They're political types, rich kids, and don't know about rip-offs.

So if you know some nut with three or four grand to burn? I won't shoot anyone. I like Turks now. But I'd much prefer a prison transfer. Thanks for the new suit. I like it.

Write
Harvey

40

Riding the Media Avalanche

In October 1978, I began the promotional tour for the film. I wanted to get out and talk about the movie, to defend it against detractors who would dismiss as Hollywood hype the reality that Harvey was still living. I thought it might help get him out. I told Columbia to set up as many interviews as they wanted and vowed to not miss a single one. It was like skiing down an avalanche. I did a sixty-day, six-country promotional tour of dawn radio interviews, morning TV talk shows, noon press luncheons, evening news shows, nightly magazine interviews, and wacky late night call-in radio shows. There were official protests by the Turkish government and heated debates about the film, drug laws, prisons, and my own credibility. There were chanting protestors carrying signs at all the film openings. Turkish protestors burned a theatre in Amsterdam. Armenian protestors demonstrated against the Turkish protestors. It all frazzled and exhausted me.

Late one afternoon during the third week of the tour, I returned to my suite at the Carlyle Hotel in Manhattan after an exhausting round of interviews. A pink message slip lay waiting on the thick brown carpet—Elizabeth Ashley was staying in the hotel and wanted me to call. We'd been introduced by a mutual friend two months before. She'd whirled into New York for a few hectic days of talk shows and interviews for her outstandingly outspoken autobiography, *Actress*.

Her voice was throaty, sensual, full of flavors and shades. "Billy, love, how are you? Congratulations and all that bullshit on the movie. Listen, to be honest, a friend can't make it to the opening of Hank Fonda's Broadway show, and I was wondering if you'd like to go with me? That is, if you're not too busy being the hot item on the celebrity circuit."

Did I want to go? Jesus, this was Elizabeth Ashley, the movie star, best actress on Broadway when she was twenty-three; "Maggie," the sizzling cat on the hot tin roof who'd heated so many of my adolescent fantasies.

"I have a limo..." I offered casually, crazy visions flashing through my feverish mind.

"Don't we all," she replied with a laugh. "No, thanks, honey. I've got my own fine driver for these occasions; he takes good care of me. Why don't you just come down to my room about seven and we'll get crazy before we leave."

The long black car glided through the busy evening traffic on Park Avenue like a deep-keeled yacht. In the plush isolation of the back seat I lit up a joint, and Elizabeth uncorked her ivory whaletooth coke holder. People on the sidewalk stared as the big car rolled past, some straining for a glimpse of the mysterious occupants behind the tinted glass.

"This is incredible," I laughed, lowering the powerglide window a crack to blow some Hawaiian smoke into the New York night. "I always used to wonder who was inside these big black mothers."

"Well, now you know. Just us drug-addled artists...or any other clown who can afford twenty-five bucks an hour."

"I don't think I'll ever get used to traveling by limousine."

"Honey," drawled Elizabeth, "don't you ever get used to it. This is half the fun, playing dress-up and riding around wrecked in these fancy hearses." We turned up 57th Street, heading for the Theatre District.

"Yeah, it beats the hell out of prison and beans. I just find it all a little hard to believe sometimes, that's all. I just got desperate enough, and escaped from prison; everything else just...seemed to happen. You know what I mean?"

She smiled and offered me the toot. "I sure do. We both know it was a lot of luck, some good timing and a fair amount of balls thrown in. But now's the hard part—you've got to move on, got to follow up to show everyone you're not just some one-shot fluke."

"Yeah, including myself."

"Especially yourself." We were in midtown, half a block from the theatre. Elizabeth beamed at me. "But, hell, you'll do it. I've got faith in you. Shit, you don't think I want any short-hitters for friends, do you?" The car stopped and I stepped out as the driver opened the door.

"Miss Ashley," I said, offering my arm.

"Well, la dee dah!" she crooned, taking hold and leading me across the street toward the crowded confusion in front of the theatre.

She was instantly recognized. Cameras flashed as we were surrounded by autograph seekers calling her name and extending their books and pens. I moved to clear a path for us, but Elizabeth tugged my hand and nodded it was all right.

"These are my people," she said, glowing. "I love 'em."

She signed and smiled and spoke with her fans, all the while moving us smoothly toward the floodlit entrance of the theatre. A few people even recognized me as "that guy who escaped from prison," and I self-consciously signed some autographs.

Cameras flashed in our faces as we entered the ornate lobby. "Elizabeth! Miss Ashley! Over here! Over here!" shouted photographers. A young woman thrust a tape recorder at us. "Miss Ashley, how long have you and Billy been seeing each other?" Elizabeth raised an eyebrow and flashed her smile, then we were through the double doors strolling arm in arm down the carpeted aisle toward the stage.

"God!" she whispered to me, "wait till you see all the rumors that start flying—'Outlaw Actress and Escaped Con'—the press will love it." Her tone turned mock serious. "I should have warned you this sort of thing might happen. They do so love to gossip about me. I hope this doesn't hurt your...reputation." She nodded and waved to friends in the celebrity-packed audience as we followed a dour-faced old usherette who'd taken the ticket stubs.

"I feel positively royal walking through here with you on my arm," I said. "Screw the gossip."

"Elizabeth, darling!" cried an older woman in black with elegantly coiffed blonde hair and the eyes and beak of an aging fish hawk. The usherette pointed out our seats and handed me the stubs. I offered her a quarter, which she looked at as if it were something fresh from my nose. "Not here," she whispered with a thin smile. I looked up and Fishhawk was watching me as Elizabeth introduced us. "Billy Hayes, recently of Istanbul, meet Irene Worth, First Lady of the Theatre."

Fishhawk turned away even before her icy "Hello..." had shriveled my embarrassed smile.

"Excuse me," I mumbled to myself, glancing around at my feet, "did I fart or something?" Elizabeth suppressed a smile and tugged my hand. The houselights blinked off and on and we all took our seats.

41

Escape to Hawaii

After two exhausting and mind-bendingly intense months of interviews, Columbia Pictures was sending me to Hawaii to recuperate.

I pulled up the steep hill below my beach apartment one evening in a black limousine and had the driver wait with the engine running. Wendy had been staying there while I was touring. I kissed her, threw some clothes in a bag, and explained that I just needed some space to get away and be alone. We got into a fight, and I yelled at her to be gone when I got back. She was crying when I left.

I was burning inside, and the driver couldn't get the emergency brake to release. I sat there fuming in the car. The driver said we could still move in reverse, and it seemed quite fitting to make my getaway backwards in a limousine.

I spent a week alone on the Kona coast, not talking to anyone, running through lava fields and swimming for hours in the blue embracing ocean; I decided to separate myself from anything connected to "Billy Hayes, *Midnight Express.*"

I desperately needed something in my life, but I wasn't sure what it was. The acting process and the relationship with Wendy both seemed to be aiming in toward the center where the pain was. I wanted to be brave and open myself to both of them, but it was so very difficult for me to trust. I'd built a shield around my emotions to survive prison—nothing got in, but nothing got out, either.

I was afraid to let anyone in to that vulnerable place where love can grow, but fortunately Wendy had pioneer woman tenacity, and her own need for the love she sensed in me. Our relationship paralleled the continuing group therapy that acting class had become—an intensely disruptive but eventually healing process.

42

Harvey Works His Plan

On a bitterly cold January morning, an old Afghani with one milky blue eye beneath a dirty black turban was leaning against the courtyard wall, staring up at tattered white clouds scudding across the wind-swept sky above Sagmalcilar prison.

"*Salaam Alayicum,*" said Harvey, sliding up beside him.

"*Alayicum salaam,*" returned Baba with a grin.

"Cigarette?" offered Harvey, shaking one from the package, then striking a match.

"Thanks," said Baba, cupping his gnarled brown hands over Harvey's and leaning into the match. Harvey flicked away the match and casually pocketed a small silver foil packet. He gave Baba the package of cigarettes, nodding at the Turkish lira folded inside.

"Keep them, my friend," said Harvey.

"Go with God," said Baba, slipping the cigarettes into his jala-ba.

"Right," grinned Harvey, turning back into the prison and continuing on toward the dispensary.

The doctor had been giving him codeine pain pills to ease his ongoing pain, but they weren't helping anymore. Harvey had been seeing him regularly and steadily increasing the weekly bribe he slipped the good doctor at each visit. Harvey wanted to establish a medical trail of evidence. He also wanted stronger medicine, and heroin had become cheap and abundant the past year. The normal supply of pills and hashish seemed to be drying up. A lot of people were snorting the white powder. He rubbed his fingers impatiently on the smooth foil in his pocket. There were more dangers to this plan than just getting shot.

February 29, 1979
Leap-year-day?

Billy,

...Thanks. The new music book mellows me. I had run out. If I have something to occupy my mind I'm OK, if not... I'm sorry I left our friendship in such a state that the only link left between us was funding a jailbreak. I didn't intend to do that. It just happened because last year was so bad... The heroin epidemic hit this place hard... We managed to throw all the junkies out of our cellblock... Had to, they kept having fits and punching out windows in the dead of winter... Couldn't let that go on.

That's where things are at here. If you have any ideas, tell me... I'm comfortable, I'm just really lonely... Nothing but Turks, Arabs, and Kurds... Georgio, who you knew, was the last good tourist left and he went free long ago... He totally lost track of his wife. Gone. Swallowed by the earth. Sad. Glad I never married...

Thanks for all the help
Harvey

March 17, 1979

Billy,

It's been a record cold winter here... Turkey had no fuel, and neither hospitals nor prisons were heated. Three prisoners died in Sagmalcilar the last week of January...

I've made friends with the prison psychologist and it should be easy for me to go to the heroin addiction section of the

*Nuthouse... it's really my only route, I can't get transferred to
any other prison... I've built a mental scam around posing as a
heavy metal junky... Who's afraid of a stumbling junky, especially if he gives you his watch and diamond ring to hold? With
the economic crisis so bad in Turkey, anyone will do anything
to make a buck... Yeah, I've survived the winter and got to get
it on now... If you can send a cheap phony diamond ring?...
There's a line of junkies flowing in and out of here going to the
hospital; I figure to step in that line, since it's moving and my
line hasn't moved in seven years... There's a heroin epidemic
here and I plan to use it as a smokescreen...*
 Love
 Harvey

All the escape plans Harvey and I had talked about came to just
that—talk. The problem was that to make anything work, we needed someone on the outside in Istanbul who we could trust and who
was knowledgeable about the ways of prison. There was only one
person who fit those qualifications, and that was me. The thought of
returning to Turkey was my worst nightmare. My dreams were
reflecting this again. I'd be back there, running from shadowy figures
with clubs while a silent scream locks in my throat. The plan for
Harvey to get transferred to the hospital as a heroin junkie had merit
in that it got him beyond the prison walls, but I worried that his
dabbling with heroin to provide a convincing excuse would get out
of control. And I worried even more that the only way to really help
him escape was for me to return to Turkey.

43

My Heart Blooms

On a brilliant spring day, at an old stone resort in the desert beyond Palm Springs, Wendy and I sat naked, facing each other, on a weathered wooden deck on a high secluded ridge. A golden sun was singing in an azure sky and snow sparkled off the surrounding mountaintops. I felt happy; alive, aware again of the purity and simplicity of existence that had overwhelmed me on that street in Amsterdam my first day of freedom. A glowing ball of light grew and pulsed in my chest. There was no need for words between us. The mountains blurred as tears of joy flowed from my eyes and the shield around my heart cracked as my light burst out and Wendy's light rushed in, flooding me with her love.

44

Harvey Gets Desperate

May 12, 1980

Hi Willie,

Consul was out and told me the two grand you sent was received. Thanks. It was a saintly gesture.

Two weeks ago, 23 prisoners escaped from the Madhouse—at one time—so I'm waiting for the action to settle down, as it were. About the same time thirteen prisoners, on route to court, seized the red courtroom bus, overpowered the soldiers, and drove off... A few days ago two guardians tried to capture a group of prisoners in the process of escaping from the roof: the prisoners tossed the guards off the roof, breaking their legs and heads and whatnot. Today the newspaper said, "OK, we're gonna start hanging anarchists." Yeah, well...as for me, I'm going to proceed with all due caution...

The cellblocks have gone crazy here due to overcrowding and smack. Smack is the new monster here, more prevalent than hash and relatively cheaper because it's smaller and easier to smuggle in. I'm taking your 1974 advice and keeping priorities in mind. I'll keep you posted. My love to you and Wendy.

Harvey

Hi Willie,   May 12, 90

        Counsul was out and told me
the 2 grand you sent was received.
Thanks. It was no less than a saintly
gesture.
        Two weeks ago 23 persons escaped from
Sakikay - at one time - so I'm waiting for
the action to settle down, as it were. About
the same time thirteen prisoners seized the
red courtroom bus, and escaped with the bus en route to count, after
overpowering the soldiers and confiscating
their arms. A few days ago two guardians
tried to capture a group of prisoners
who were in the process of escaping
from the roof; the prisoners tossed the
guards off the roof, breaking their
legs and heads and whatnot.
        Today the newspaper said "OK, we're
gonna start hanging anarchists." Yeah,
well....
        As for me, I'm going to proceed with
all due caution. The counsul, a friend,
is helpful so I don't have the problem
of dragging all that bread around on
my person. Don't expect amazing things

May 18, 1980

Hi Billy,

It's Thursday, just had an interesting visit from the Consul... He's working with the prison shrink to send me to the Narcotic Rehab section of the Madhouse for treatment of my "heroin addiction"... He's also working on getting me a special amnesty for heroin addiction...

So I'll wait and see if they send me to the hospital. Your two grand arrived last week. Consul will hold it outside until I need it delivered. This talk about a special amnesty for smack addiction is the best news I've heard, a faint hope I might be on to something... Consul is a righteous guy and thinks I am a King Kong junky.

Don't sweat all this "junky addict" shit—I'm not cut out to be a junky. You're studying acting, right? So am I. Sometimes the theatre here is a little too realistic but it's got to be to work. I can still crank off 30 pushups. I'm down from 50 last year but theatre takes its toll.

Thanks much for the bread. It makes a nice safety net beneath this greasy tightrope.

Love
Harvey

June 10, 1980

Hi Billy,

It's been a month since I "turned myself in for heroin addiction" and began trying to get to the hospital. But my adversary, the public prosecutor, is dead set against it. Turkey is also very embarrassed about heroin in prisons here and I'm the first foreigner since Max to turn myself in for "heroin addiction". To exert pressure I wrote Jack Anderson, the columnist, and told him I was strung out and asked him to help get me some place where I can receive medical attention. Now my wheels are spinning, mired in the mud and I hope this doesn't backfire on me. I dread my family might learn I'm a "junky".

I'm telling you this because I'm afraid you might think I conned you into footing the bill for a split scene when I had no intention of splitting... It might have worked last year but might not work now... It's hard for me to believe they can refuse me medical treatment. Maybe they've spied and know I'm "bluffing". I dread that they might rush in and give me a blood test before I had a chance to pollute it... But I'm still raising hell with them...

> *My love to you and Wendy*
> *Harvey*

July 19, 1980

Billy,

    I've been trying to write you a letter for days and keep tearing them up... Billy, all my efforts to get to the hospital have been unsuccessful... And in an effort to successfully fake my addiction, I became a junky... Not mainlining heroin but sniffing it like cocaine and in no way being secretive about it... So three months ago I told the Consul I was hooked and needed help. I turned myself in to the prison doctor. Fuck, I shouldn't have bothered. Billy, I have terrible guilt feelings about blowing the money you sent me but the fact is this place is outta hand and if Jesus hizself were here now he might be mainlining just to cope... I'm getting gray hairs and looking bad and feeling worse... I'm doing 36 years and these bastards are force-feeding us with heroin. Chrome-glass hypodermic syringes lying about like paper weights and guardians shuffling in and out with fat packets of smack. Outta hand. Nobody cares...Iran and Iraq just went to war...No one cares. The Turks won't send me to a hospital and the only person who is going to help me kick this mild habit I purposefully inflicted upon myself...is myself. Half the Tourist cellblock is strung out. The Turk cellblock is even worse. Billy, I believe the Embassy is blocking my attempt to get to a hospital because your book and film upset Turk-U.S. relations, to say the least. But this leaves me out in the cold. I'm naive, I never expected my own country to forsake me for political expediency. But I've got to kick this and got to get out of Sagmalcilar to do that. This place is boiling. Now I find myself taking heroin not so much to satisfy an addiction but to simply calm my nerves... I tried to stop but my body freaked out so rather than suffer alone in this madhouse I started up again... Billy, it's Dodge City in here and somebody shot the sheriff... I have a good knife but could use a scalpel blade if you got one...

How am I? Billy, I'm O.K. Thin but thinking straight. Dealing with the habit by reduction, i.e., tapering off. It's no great problem: "junky" is really a personality. I'm not of that personality type so I can leave it...

How fucking sick of this place I am, and disgusted at myself for not being able to get me out...

Maybe there'll be an Amnesty for Ataturk's birthday in 1981. That's the current fantasy/catchword—1981. I'm in Limbo. This has to change. Too weird to continue...

Love, Harvey

45

Wedding Day

Wendy and I were married by the koi pond in the lush backyard of the old house we'd bought near the beach. Scores of loved ones from all over the country came to support us. Barbara telegrammed from Switzerland, wishing us peace and a long life together.

The house had been built fifty years earlier by a Norwegian stonemason, who'd created a terraced cactus garden that trailed down the sloping lot to a little grotto pond and a small, tree-shaded

lawn. An early morning shower gave way to a sparkling bright day, and by the time the guests had arrived, the fleeting giant yellow bloom of an aged cactus above the pond was in full flower.

Dr. Bill Hornaday, affectionately known as Uncle Bill, was a magical old minister from the Church of Religious Science. He performed a warm, eloquent ceremony that lovingly acknowledged and embraced the full range of all of our various spiritual views.

Nothing in my life ever felt so right as standing there with Wendy in Uncle Bill's shining gaze, surrounded by so many of the people I loved.

46

They Didn't Like the Movie

A month after returning from our Hawaiian honeymoon, Wendy and I were drinking our morning coffee in the breakfast nook that looked out toward the ocean when the phone rang. It was Sam Gunderson, my contact at the State Department in Washington.

"Billy, listen, I hate to tell you this, but we've just had a request from the Turkish government for your extradition."

"What?"

"Yeah. They've asked for the extradition and issued an Interpol warrant for your arrest."

"Jesus Christ! What does this mean?" I saw the worry in Wendy's eyes.

"Well, don't worry," said Sam, "the U.S. isn't going to honor the extradition request, but the Interpol warrant will mean you'll have to be very careful about where you travel. Different countries have different responses to these warrants. Best thing we can recommend is that you don't leave the United States, at least until we can clear this up."

I was stunned. "Jesus, Sam, I'm out nearly five years now. Why'd they wait so long to issue a warrant?"

"I guess they didn't like the movie."

There was a long silence while I stared at Wendy, a cold fear running up my backbone.

"You just hang in there and be careful, okay?"

"Right, Sam, I'll talk to you later. Thanks for calling, I guess."

I explained the situation to Wendy and she wrapped me in her arms. I broke away and moved to the closet. She watched as I pulled down a dusty black leather case, slid open the zipper, and removed the Browning 9mm automatic pistol.

Tears slowly filled her eyes.

47

Harvey Gets Hooked

August 8, 1980

Hello Billy,
    ...Heroin has put me in a terrible funk. When I stop I get suicidally depressed. Can't get any help kicking. Doctors don't care. Embassy doesn't care. And not only does the Prison administration not care how many prisoners get desperately strung out but someone is making a lot of money on our misery.
    But I care... At least I never got into mainlining, just sniffing it up my nose. But as Wm. Burroughs once noted, it doesn't matter if you shoot it, snort it, or stuff it up your ass, the end result is still the same: addiction...
    I never would have believed addiction is such a total condition, that it invades every cranny of the body and brain. But the majority of the discomfort is mental: nothing has ever sent me into such depths of psychological depression before...
    In the past weeks I've been trying to kick. I had to lay out a lot of bread on kicking medicine.
    I'd like to tell you that I'm forever cured but I'm not that naive. I wish I could get myself to another place where the stuff isn't available. The reason I got on smack in the first place is the sheer intolerability of this cellblock system—the continual noise and hassles with illiterate Arabs... I'm still a shaky case but I'm

a hell of a lot better than I was... Perhaps a quarter of this cell-block is strung-out... People sell their clothes, watches, rings, radios—anything of value—to buy heroin. I never felt sorry for junkies before, I do now. I couldn't sleep for the nightmares— still can't...

Yes, well, I could wait to see how my "health problem" develops before sending this letter but since I am myself in suspense you might as well be also. At least my heart's in the right place—I've done all I can to help me stop the stuff—the spirit is weak after all the years in here...

...I hope you and Wendy had a wonderful honeymoon. Once I spent a few fantastic days in Hawaii and the land was so lush it had a psychedelic aura.

Anyway, Billy, Wendy, I love you both. You two are like a beacon out there on a stormy night.

Harvey

48

Tennessee Williams

I'm too old to lifeguard, and my profile is too high to smuggle, so I've become an actor."

By October of 1981 that's what I semi-seriously told people curious about my life after the *Midnight Express* madness. But I had become an actor, and for the past year now, Wendy and I had been working with Eric Morris and his small, tightly knit acting company in Los Angeles. We'd been rehearsing Tennessee Williams' classic play, *The Glass Menagerie*. Wendy was producing, and we'd raised money and made deposits on a theatre; in a week I was to make my theatrical debut as the Gentleman Caller.

Except that Tennessee Williams' agents had just denied us the rights to the play, which was why I found myself bleary-eyed and exhausted as the night flight from L.A. touched down in Miami. A slow-rolling wave of doubt washed over me, and I wondered what the fuck I was doing here. Was I really meeting with Tennessee Williams to ask his help in fighting ICM, the huge agency that represented him? Could I really pull this off, for myself and all the other actors depending on me?

I'd know soon enough, as I stumbled out to an old prop plane for the connecting flight to Key West. A crusty pilot in a rumpled blue uniform secured the door behind me once I entered the empty cabin. "Just us," he said, "might as well sit up front with me." Might as well, I thought, collapsing into the seat beside him. "Strap up good," he grinned, "this one should be a doozy."

My brain wasn't up to speed yet, but I didn't like the sound of that. I tried to ask him about a doozy, but my voice was drowned out by the rattling and clattering as we rumbled down the runway then *lurched* into the slick dawn sky. A little moan squeaked out of me, and I thought I heard the pilot laugh.

"Wheee," he said, as the plane bucked and shuddered. "You're lucky, this is probably the last flight out today, what with the turbulence." My stomach was full of wriggling eels.

"Turbulence? What turbulence?" I asked, shouting above the throbbing engines.

"That's the spirit," he cackled, mistaking my fearful question for bravado. "Hurricane Katrina, they're callin' her, building there beyond Cuba." I followed his gaze out the window to a line of huge dark clouds gathering like bull elephants on the horizon. "Should be here in forty-eight hours. Flights'll all be shuttin' down, 'fraid of the storm, but I love to fly in this weather." I was alone in the plane with this obvious lunatic, I had no parachute, and we were heading for the eye of a hurricane. All right, this was beginning to feel like Tennessee Williams country.

An hour later we touched down on the tiny Key West runway. The air was thick, moist and fragrant. A soft drizzle began to fall as I cruised my rusty rented Honda past shabby houseboats snugged in along mangrove-lined lagoons on one side, and stately white houses wrapped with trellises of rampant red bougainvillea on the other.

On LaRue Street, beneath towering cypress trees, I rented a corner room off a wide veranda in an old mansion called the Banyan House. I stripped off my damp clothes and stood beneath a slowly spinning ceiling fan, then collapsed onto the cool sheets of the four-poster bed. A saxophone was swaying softly somewhere nearby, and a faint drawling voice on a radio was speaking about a lady named "Katrina" building in the Gulf and heading for the Keys. Thunder rumbled in the distance, and on the slippery edge of sleep I laughed again to think that this was so like being in a Tennessee Williams play.

I woke at noon, surprised, covered with sweat, not a clue as to where I was. A lazy fan spun overhead…it was coming back now…I was in Key West to talk with Tennessee Williams, America's greatest playwright. Could that be right?

I toweled off after a cold shower, then found the phone number I'd gotten from Captain Tony, an infamous Key West character who Wendy had recently met while working on a film based on his exploits called *Key West Crossing*. Tony knew everyone and owned Captain Tony's Saloon, where he used to drink with Papa Hemingway. When I called the number, a deep, cultured voice answered. It was Frank, Tennessee's secretary/housekeeper. When I introduced myself he informed me "T.W." was at the doctor's and asked me to call back later. I set my alarm for four and plopped back into bed.

At four, T.W. himself answered. "Oh yes," he said, in soft, graveled-honey tones, "I remember you well, from the movie. You're beautiful." He was confusing me with Brad Davis. I explained the difference and his voice flooded with emotion. "Oh, my child, you're the real one who was in that terrible prison?"

"Yes."

"Well, I truly feel for you and your family. I congratulate you on getting out." He began coughing and held the phone away from his mouth. "Excuse me, I'm not feeling too well today."

"Should I call back another time, sir?"

"Yes. Would you mind? Call me tonight at seven, after the news. I'm a news addict, so call me after the news at seven."

When I called at seven, T.W.'s speech was slurred, and he sounded drained. I could hear shouting in the background. "Billy, I am sorry, but there's some trouble here this evening. Let me call you tomorrow."

I was relieved. I'd rather meet him fresh, during the day. Tony had told me he was sharper by day and usually fried by sundown. I drove to Mallory Square, the southern tip of America, and watched a muted orange sun drown in dark purple clouds. I'd made contact with T.W., but I felt nervous and incomplete, and the storm was coming. I found an old, weathered phone booth on the worn wooden dock and called Wendy. I was reassured by the sound of her voice, though distressed to hear that we'd just paid $2,500 more to secure our rental of the Callboard Theatre and that the cast remained despondent about the rights.

I felt pressured and fatigued as I walked back to the car. A steady rain began to fall, and the fleeting possibility of failure rippled like icy water down my spine. My uneasiness increased when I reached the car to find I'd locked the keys inside. All attempts to jimmy the door failed.

I huddled in the phone booth for an hour until a locksmith arrived and opened the door in the downpour. I drove to the Banyan House on automatic pilot then fell into a deep sleep and dreamed my father and I were together on a long, slow train…

Next morning, I had a late breakfast of croissants, coffee, orange juice, and anxiety beside the small, leaf-strewn pool. I waited for the phone call while a mass of dark clouds loomed over the southern horizon. A large, tanned dumpling in a tiny black swimsuit tried to make conversation from the next lounge chair, but I politely ignored him, so he returned to the aging German countess lying topless beside him. I heard the mellow sax floating somewhere in the trees.

"That's the guy from Spyro Gyra," said Justin, the pool boy, swishing out from the house. He collected some dishes then struck a pose in front of us. "Anyone want anything?" he asked, with what had to be an Italian salami stuffed into his white string swimsuit. "No? Well, just call." And he was gone with a wink.

Noon passed. One o'clock. One-thirty. I called T.W.'s house. Frank answered—he was sympathetic and told me T.W. was lunching at the Pier House. My uneasiness increased. I decided action was called for and drove to the restaurant.

I saw T.W. at a far table with a solid, fiftyish blonde woman and an agitated young Englishman, whose long brown ponytail flopped about as he voiced his complaints in a cultured whine. "I've always been rich, goddamn it, and I've never been happy a day in my life!"

T.W. gently reached for his hand, but Ponytail shrugged him off and ranted louder. "I'm not a baby! Stop babying me!"

This seemed an inopportune time for introductions. I ordered coffee and watched from a nearby table. The Englishman raved on while T.W. listened patiently. He looked old and tired. He adjusted his thick, black horn-rimmed glasses, sipped some red wine, then rested his silvered beard on his hand. Just once his face lit up with a smile, and a deep, delicious laugh bubbled out of him.

When they rose to leave, Ponytail headed for the restroom and I hurried outside. T.W. emerged, a smallish figure with hands deep in his pea coat pockets and a little blue captain's cap snugged down on his white head. I stepped in front of him.

"Excuse me, Mr. Williams, I'm Billy Hayes."

He was startled, then recognized my name. "Oh, yes, forgive me for not calling you." I took his extended hand—it felt chilled and fragile.

"No, please, I apologize for intruding on you like this." We stared at each other a moment, then the blonde woman exited the restaurant and moved protectively to T.W.'s side. "Helen," he said, still holding my hand, "this is Billy Hayes."

"Ahh..." chimed Helen, relaxing, bathing me in a huge smile.

"Helen takes care of me," he offered. We stood there silently, and I could feel both of them examining me, sensing me with highly tuned antennae.

"I just need a moment, sir, to speak with you about *The Glass Menagerie.*"

"Billy," said Helen, "why not follow us back to the house. You and Tom can sit by the pool and work this out."

T.W. nodded, still smiling at me.

Ponytail burst through the doors. There was a butter knife held low in his left hand. "Billy Hayes," Helen quickly began, "this is Robert—"

"*Mister* Robert Carroll," he shouted at me, "heir to the Carroll banking fortune, and I'm rich, bloody fucking rich!! Are you?!"

At lunch I'd noted the ferret-like movements of his thin body, and up close I could see his pupils were dark pinpoints. Still, I was surprised by his intensity and blurted out the first thing that came to me. "Well, I'm rich in spirit."

He sneered and said, "You look stupid," dismissing me with a glance and turning away. An adrenaline surge sent my right hand twitching toward his poncey little ponytail, but I checked the impulse. "And you look rude," I shouted at his retreating back. A quick glance showed me T.W. was aware of everything, intently focused on the scene.

"I look *what?*" said Robert, turning about.

"Rude," I replied, my body tensing for his response. The possibility of a fight was always a scary rush, even when you're dealing with a skinny junkie holding a butter knife.

"Of course I'm rude, you bloody fool, I can afford to be rude. It comes from being rich."

"It comes from being insecure."

He jerked as if stung by a bee. "I'm not insecure!" he screamed, waving the knife in the air. "I'm bloody fucking rich, and if you don't disappear instantly I'll cut your fucking balls off."

A sputter of sound from T.W.

"That's right, laugh, you bastard! You're loving this."

"Robert..." said T.W.

"Don't 'Robert' me! How'd you like it if I cut my bleeding throat with this knife? You'd be happy to be rid of me, wouldn't you?!" He wheeled around and charged back into the restaurant.

Helen took our arms and led us to a weathered little Datsun. "Robert has some problems," she said. "Just ignore him and follow us home. I'll distract Robert while you and Tom talk."

I crossed the parking lot to my car. Robert returned to the Datsun and sat up front beside Helen. There was shouting and loud arguing. As Helen got out and approached me, I knew the meeting was postponed again.

"I'm sorry," she said, "he's really impossible, and so draining on Tom. Could we meet you here at seven for dinner? We're putting Robert on the six o'clock flight."

I understood, I'd lived around junkies in prison. I looked to the dark sky and hoped Hurricane Katrina wouldn't close the airport. I looked back and Robert was sprinting wildly across the parking lot toward my car. He skidded to a halt just five feet from the driver's door and glared at me with crazed eyes. His thin body was quivering with rage. I cocked my left arm as he stepped toward the open window and hissed at me, "If I *ever* see your face around here again, I'll kill you!"

He leapt back as the door swung open and I surged out. I heard Helen shout, "Don't hurt him!" but I wasn't sure who she meant.

"Listen, Jack," I snarled, struggling for control, "you better find out who you're dealing with or you're gonna get hurt—bad!"

The effect on Robert was startling. All the tension left his body and a huge, silly smile creased his ascetic face. "*Jack*," he trilled, to no one in particular, "he called me... Jack!" Then he turned and floated serenely back toward the Datsun.

Katrina seemed to be lingering off Cuba. The muggy afternoon lay dead still awaiting her arrival. With time to kill before my dinner meeting with T.W., I found myself sitting against a towering magnolia tree beside a long rococo swimming pool in Ernest Hemingway's backyard. I was surrounded by cats—scores of them roamed the lush grounds around the vine-covered villa that was now a museum and tourist attraction. The kindly black guard at the front door had informed me the cats were all descendants of Papa's cats and were cared for according to instructions in his will.

I was the only visitor today. I'd just stood for an hour at the roped-off entrance to Papa's writing room, staring at the old Remington typewriter that sat faithfully on the high ledge of a massive wooden desk, awaiting the touch of a large man who worked standing on his feet. I wondered about inspiration, dedication, and the shotgun in Idaho.

It was quiet against the tree beside the pool. The water level was low and swampy, green with algae and fallen leaves. A small frog popped to the surface, then hopped up onto a mossy step. His googly eyes swiveled around, and we stared at each other before a gray cat leapt from the rhododendron bushes and pounced on the frog. The cat shifted its paws, and the frog splurted back into the pool. "Almost," I said to the cat, who took it well, settling down to stare at the water and wait.

"So, Billy," said T.W. a few hours later, as Helen helped settle him into a chair, "was it really as awful as the movie?" His bright blue eyes were bloodshot but alert behind the thick glasses. The Pier House was nearly empty, and a rising wind splattered occasional raindrops against the windows beside us. I was nervous and a little guilty about T.W. coming out in this weather.

"Well, emotionally it was pretty accurate, but they changed a lot of things."

"Yes, don't they always. You wrote the film?"

"No, sir, I wrote the book. Oliver Stone wrote the film."

"But all that happened to you?"

"Pretty much."

"The beatings and such?"

"Tom," intervened Helen, "maybe he doesn't want to talk about it."

"Oh, forgive me," said T.W., "I was just...curious."

"No, that's all right. I'm used to it. Everyone's curious."

"You were there how long?"

"Five years—from 1970 to 1975."

"My god. And didn't they send you to a madhouse where you killed that brutish guard and escaped?"

"The madhouse scene was very close to reality, but the escape was changed completely."

"So you didn't kill the guard and steal the keys?"

"No, sir, the guard was shot by another inmate a year earlier, and I escaped from a different prison, off an island in a rowboat in a storm."

"Your manners are impeccable, but do call me Tom."

"All right, Tom."

"Well, that ending certainly sounds more exciting and cinematic."

"It was. But Alan Parker, the director, wasn't interested in the escape as much as making a film about hope and fear and not giving up."

"I think he succeeded. Are you pleased with it?"

"Yes, for the most part. I have some problems, but I'm the least objective of viewers. The Turks aren't so happy."

"I should think not—they come across as quite barbaric."

"That's one of my main problems with the movie—you don't see a single good Turk, so they all look bad. Which, of course, isn't true."

"Of course." T.W. stared at me. "You certainly don't look like a hard-time convict. He has the face of an angel, doesn't he, Helen?"

"Yes," said Helen, smiling at me as I shifted around in my chair.

"And an athlete's body," said T.W. "Billy, I'd love to do a painting of you, naked beside the pool."

Naked beside the pool? Jesus! How much do I have to give for my art?

"I really should paint him, don't you think, Helen?"

"Yes, Tom, you should, but Billy, you have some problem with *The Glass Menagerie*, isn't that right?"

"Yes. We've been rehearsing for months—"

"Are you acting now?" asked T.W.

"Yes. This'll be my first time on stage—the Gentleman Caller."

"How wonderful."

"Except that we've put up money for the theatre and other expenses, and now we can't get the rights to do the play."

"Why not? It's done everywhere."

"I know, 281 times in the U. S. last year. Everyone loves your play—but our production is going to be different. The director, Eric Morris, has wanted to do a real version for twenty years, to show an Amanda with the guts to survive hard times alone with two children—"

"Are you always this hyper?" T.W. asked.

"I just think he's excited meeting you," said Helen.

"Yes, sir, it's really a thrill for me. I love your work...Tom."

"Thank you, Billy, your praise is gratifying, but do have some wine and relax. You can be a bit overwhelming."

"Sorry, I get revved up."

"I noticed. Robert usually out-blusters most people."

"I'm sorry if I caused problems."

"No, he's just insanely jealous and...sick."

"A lot of people were sick like that in prison. It makes life difficult."

"For everyone involved," said T.W., smiling at me. "And what are your indulgences these days?"

"Well, I did a lot of drugs back in the Sixties."

"Ah, yes, the Sixties, I've forgotten them well."

"But now I'm pretty straight, except for an occasional joint. Do a lot of long distance running, marathons and stuff." I sipped some wine. "I don't even like alcohol, but it's an honor to drink with you."

That delicious laugh bubbled out of him again. "There are those who would consider it something less than an honor. You're very kind."

We sat quietly for a moment while the wind rattled the windows.

"So, are you a health nut? You certainly look healthy, doesn't he, Helen?"

Helen smiled at me. "You do look wonderful for having been in prison all those years."

"Well, I'm happy and in love and life is real sweet for me these days."

"What would you do," asked T.W. slowly, "if you knew you were going to die? Knew it. And very soon?" He fixed me with bright blue eyes, sunken now in the weathered folds of his face. I had a fleeting image of an old holy man sitting in a high mountain cave staring at a setting sun.

"I'm fascinated by death," I said. "What is it? What happens? I mean, I'm not ready to leave *this* yet, whatever this is, but I'm curious about what, if anything, is next. I figure it's something or nothing—and if it's nothing, you have nothing to worry about; and if it's something, then what is it?"

"It's nothing," T.W. said sadly.

"But what about our energy, our life-force continuing somehow, our body fading but our consciousness going on...?"

T.W. turned from the table as a hacking cough racked his body. After the spasm he asked, "Are you religious?"

"I was raised Catholic, but left the church after puberty created some major differences of opinion."

"It can certainly do that."

"I still have no use for organized religion, but I guess I'm more spiritual now."

"Spiritual...so you found God in prison?"

"Something like that."

"He seems to frequent those environs."

"Well, I got into yoga and meditation, learned about heart chakras and the God within all of us..."

T.W. let me prattle on awhile then gently asked, "How old are you?"

I suddenly felt quite foolish, and my embarrassment must have shown because he added, "That's all right, the Gentleman Caller is also an optimist."

"So why can't you do the play?" asked Helen.

"Right, the play, thank you. When we applied to the Dramatists Guild for rights, we were told ICM was considering a Tennessee Williams revival next year in L.A., so all rights were being withheld."

"They thought you'd be competition."

"Right, but we wouldn't be. This is a little Equity-waiver production! And besides, we love this play, we've been working on it in class for six months, we've paid for the theatre..."

"All right," said T.W., "calm down. It's just agents. Have you tried calling them?"

"I did. It took awhile, but I got through and explained our situation. No one really cared."

"That's always the problem, isn't it? Well, don't worry, I'll call them, I'll talk with them."

That's what I wanted to hear! "So then I should wait until the Dramatists Guild contacts us about the rights?"

"Don't wait for anything!" shouted T.W., rising and leaning forward on the table. "I wrote the damn play and I'm telling you, do the play!"

"Yes, sir," I said, beaming, coming around the table to shake his hand and get embraced. His gray whiskers were brittle against my cheek, but there was still strength in his thin frame. He held me at arm's length and twirled a lock of my blonde hair on his finger. "Yes," he said, "I must paint you. Come to the house tomorrow for breakfast and I'll paint you beside the pool."

Hurricane Katrina was moving in, and the island was battening down when I arrived at T.W.'s house next morning. He was in his silk maroon robe and blue slippers and seemed to have taken a turn for the worse. I had my suitcase in hand and suggested cutting the meeting short. We embraced in the doorway and he said, "I'll have to paint you another time."

"I'd be honored." And I meant it. "Thank you."

"Well, God bless you and don't worry about anything. Just do the play."

I caught the last flight out, raced the storm to Miami and connected through to Los Angeles. Back at the theatre, everyone was excited by the news, and I felt the joy of an adventure completed.

A week later, two days before opening night, I was sitting alone on the steps of the Callboard Theatre during a rehearsal break when a telegram arrived from ICM. It informed us they'd been in touch with T.W. and that he now refused us permission to do *The Glass Menagerie* and that they were prepared to contact Actors' Equity and bend us over in court if we proceeded with our production. I walked back into the theatre, slowly crumpling the telegram into a small yellow ball.

"So, we ready to start again?" asked Eric, clapping his hands.

"Yeah, sure," I said, placing the yellow ball into the torn but neatly mended pocket of the Gentleman Caller's sport coat. "Let's do the play...do the play!"

We did the play. I never told the cast, we never heard from ICM, and there never was a revival in Los Angeles. The next time I saw T.W. was three years later—he was laid out in a coffin in a New York funeral parlor. I thought he looked good, at peace. I laid a rose in the coffin and whispered to him, "Something or nothing?"

49

The Plot Thickens

Harvey's situation had become intolerable. My own happiness seemed a constant cruel reminder of his miserable condition. All the escape plans we'd discussed seemed insane, but that sort of goes with the territory. I began to seriously consider the reality of returning to Turkey and taking my best shot at freeing Harvey.

An ally in this was Jon, a West Point graduate who'd been involved in Black Ops in Vietnam, later worked as a mercenary, and was hungry for a new adventure. I trusted his heart, and he was definitely the kind of guy you want around in a tight situation.

The plan with the most merit involved transferring Harvey from the Istanbul prison to one outside Izmir, near an American Army base where he could receive better medical attention. We thought this could be arranged, and I knew the method of transfer would involve Harvey and two soldiers in a prison van, driving the 500 kilometers from Istanbul to Izmir. Jon and I would enter Turkey by ferry from the tiny Greek island of Samos, which sits just off the Turkish coastline, a few miles south of Izmir. I would dye my hair. We'd have false passports and scuba equipment with us, ostensibly to enjoy the great diving for which the region is famous. At a pre-arranged point, Jon and I would engage the van, disable the soldiers and make our way to the beach with Harvey. We'd don the waiting scuba equipment and swim five kilometers to Samos, and freedom. We were clear that killing the guards was not an option, or we'd be

→ forget the beads. The Youngster knows the doctor, the hospital orderlies. But to pay off the hospital orderlies, doctor — to set it up - he'll need a quarter, half million lira. Two and three dollar scams are desperate moves.

$10,000 = 500,000 lira · 20 grand = 1 million lira.

[Dec 7]

That's how much it costs to do it and get away. Julian was a Turk doing his [who knows] escape in a foreigner. Pay the mob, watch everybody smile and walk off. It's all a matter of money.

[Dear Willie] — This is another P.S. to the letter I sent you yesterday. This is called: Second Thoughts. Listen: if you know someone _smart_ who can come here and bring some money without being eaten by a _shark_ then I know someone who can set the whole thing up where I literally walk from my cell and two or three days later quietly go to a house and disappear, or yes, fly right out of the country. But two things are imperative: one, that the man ~~doesn't~~ your courier has to deal with is a man-eating shark who, if your courier isn't smart, will gobble him like a guppy, and second, that were talking about minimum half a million lira, ten thousand dollars, which is the smallest sharkbait Youngster Ahmet Tashpinar would react to. But he can do the whole thing like a Swiss watch. It's this, willie...money...a half million lira is the smallest negociable currency at this level. There are guys all over Istanbul who owe Ahmet Tashpinar half a million lira. When they don't pay him he shoots them. He wears 600 suits and he's a certified ~~psy~~ psycopath. He's also a gentleman. If it goes through me he won't rip me off. He can't. His son and brother are in this gail at this moment. If it goes through his son then he is ripping off his own family, himself, in fact. The Youngster knows me well enough to believe I'd cut his son Hasan's ~~throat~~ ~~cut~~ throat (which I really couldn't imagine myself doing because Hasan is really a nice kid: he wouldn't rip me off. neither would Ahmet if his honor and his sons

— JS'd any

[left margin, vertical text]: Willie, this is the last part of this letter. I shot this [what so handles the this] before being outside and just greasing palms full of walk-but-because [wrought-thinking] in ten or twenty of thousand of dollars stirring, just a matter of paying the money without getting one hundred fifty cents off and paying my pants off, and having a courier [...]

wanted men everywhere in the world—not to mention the karmic implications. This made the plan even more difficult.

Wendy was vaguely aware that we were talking escape plans with Harvey, but didn't take it seriously. The insanity of the plan, and the fact that I was keeping the growing reality of it from her, showed how far I still had to go to learn the lessons and heal the effects of my long imprisonment and escape.

50

Reunion and Redemption

I was saved from making another potentially huge mistake when Sam Gunderson called from the State Department late one night with stunning news. The long-awaited Prisoner Exchange Treaty had finally been enacted. Harvey Bell and the three other Americans imprisoned in Turkey were on their way home. They'd be at Kennedy Airport the following morning. Sam explained that under the terms of the treaty, they would be on parole here in America for the remainder of their sentences. There was a special clause in the treaty that forbade them from associating with one another when they got home, and none of them were allowed to publicly speak about their time in Turkey or write anything about it. This was an obvious reference to me and *Midnight Express*. Sam thought it would hurt Harvey if I was at the airport. I reluctantly agreed.

When the Americans got off the plane at Kennedy, they were mobbed by reporters. Their statements to the press were brief, but they were asked about *Midnight Express* and the effect it might have had on them. The two American women denounced me, the book and the movie, stating that my selfish actions had caused the Turkish government to backlash and, in effect, kept them in prison for several more years than were necessary. They thought the pressure from *Midnight Express* did them more harm than good, and that I was a selfish ingrate who only cared about himself. I read all this with only mild upset. Harvey knew the truth, and he was home!

They were held in the Manhattan Detention Center for a week after returning, while paperwork and preparations for further action were taken care of. Harvey was to be returned to Alabama, his home, where he'd be remanded to the custody of the local authorities who'd arranged the terms of his probation.

My dad went to the Center to visit Harvey and offer what help he could. Dad called me after the meeting to say that Harvey was in pretty bad physical condition but still gnarly and very happy to be out of Turkey. Dad said Harvey felt bitter about the manner of his return and the harsh parole restrictions that seemed to be forthcoming. He was free, but there were a lot of extenuating conditions. I felt bad for Harvey but had to laugh at his attitude. No one could break his rebellious spirit.

Two weeks later I received a phone call. Harvey was in San Diego, clearing up some legal issues. Wendy and I drove down from Los Angeles, and rang him from the lobby of his little waterfront hotel. I found I was nervous after the long years that had passed since we'd seen each other. But then the elevator doors opened, and he was sauntering across the lobby wearing his beat-up old boots and a huge shitkickin' grin on his skinny face. We shook and embraced, feeling both awkward and overjoyed. He kissed Wendy and thanked her for the years of letters and support.

Over dinner and wine and coffee we wiled away the evening with talk and laughter and an occasional tear. It felt strange to both of us to be together again and free, Outside where we'd dreamed of being for so long. The long years showed in Harvey's face, but his eyes still sparkled, and no matter what the future held in store, he was ready for it. He apologized for what the others had said to the media. He told me that I'd never been anything less than a true friend. This was a redemption of sorts for me. We all felt thankful to be alive.

51

The Midnight Express Experience

October, 1983: Outside Amherst College in New Jersey, the gray drizzle became a downpour as I stepped from the cab. I had a small travel umbrella that Wendy had insisted I take along, but the ivy-covered buildings were far across an expanse of green lawn, so I clutched my shoulder bag and ducked beneath the shelter of an ancient tree. It was dry and snug. There were posters tacked up all over the massive trunk. I saw my face staring out from behind bars on one of them and had to laugh.

It was an hour until my lecture was scheduled to start, so I stared out at the curtain of rain, centering myself, enjoying the isolation…

I'd avoided talking publicly about *Midnight Express* for years now. Then in January, while acting in a New York production of *Bent* (Martin Sherman's powerful play about Dachau concentration camp) I had a call from John Oltran, a student at my alma mater, Marquette University. John wanted me to come to Milwaukee and speak. I wanted to know how John got my unlisted phone number.

"I'm very resourceful," he said. "I hope you don't mind. I don't want to bug you, but a couple of us were bullshitting over some brews at the Avalanche—"

"The Avalanche is still there?" I asked.

"Oh, yeah—pool tables, derelicts, the works."

"Is Mike still there?"

"The little guy looked like Groucho Marx? Nah, he died a couple of years ago."

Too bad. Mike had given me my first beer in Milwaukee back in 1964. The drinking age had been twenty-one, my phony I.D. said I was twenty-three, and I looked about fourteen.

"Anyway," John continued, "you're like Marquette's most famous alumni, and we'd love to have you come back and speak about the *Midnight Express* stuff."

"I think the word is infamous, John, and I'm an actor now, I don't do that anymore. Besides, I'm doing a play. I can't leave New York."

"Well, how about when the play is over?"

"John, if I changed my number, you'd probably find the new one, wouldn't you?"

"Well, I am persistent."

"And I happen to be the kind of guy who especially appreciates that quality."

"I know that, which is why I'm persisting here beyond the point of courtesy, perhaps, but I still think it's a great idea. We couldn't pay you much, but we'd pick up expenses, and I know you'd pack the Varsity."

"I'd be speaking in the Varsity?"

Boiinnggg! Deep echoing gongs of memory.

"The old Varsity Theatre, where they used to have those oddball classes during the day, that's still there?" Daydreaming through some rinky-dink Music Appreciation class on an April afternoon, then hustling girls down there on Friday nights—cheap thrills and popcorn.

"Yeah," said John, "I know its old and funky, but it holds a crowd, and there would definitely be one."

This kid had me intrigued. He'd zeroed in on my nostalgia buttons. "John, I'm finished this play in a month. Call me in a month, we'll talk."

"So you'll do it?"

"Call me, okay?"

"Okay."

"Don't lose that number, now."

"Thanks."

John called back, and one night in March I found myself backstage at the Varsity Theatre, pacing the worn wooden floorboards, aware of the huge, buzzing crowd just beyond the massive blue curtains. John had been right—the place was packed, every seat full, people sitting in the aisles and standing in the rear. I was nervous, doing breathing exercises and taking emotional inventories like I'd learned from Eric Morris. I'd done a lot of stage work since 1979, but this was different—this was talking about *Midnight Express* and the personal stuff again. I also had no idea what I was going to say, but that had never stopped me before. I heard John tapping the microphone, asking the noisy house to settle down.

"In October 1970, Billy Hayes, a former Marquette student (some cheers) was arrested at the Istanbul airport (some boos) while attempting to smuggle four pounds of hashish out of Turkey (wild cheers and applause)". Right off I could tell this was going to be a rowdy crowd. I felt better.

"He wrote a book about his experience, *Midnight Express,* which was made into a film, and he's here tonight to talk about it. I give you…Billy Hayes."

The warmth and empathy of the crowd, the fond memories of college days in the Sixties—a time before my world changed—made it feel like a homecoming for me. I was able to speak openly and honestly—several times affected to the point of tears—and it was all right, great, in fact. I realized I must be healing and felt such relief and joy that it swelled over and infected the crowd. I talked for hours, answering and asking questions, laughing and bullshitting with old friends who'd pop up in the audience. A former roommate introduced me to a seventeen-year-old clone of himself, who he swore was his son, the freshman, but I knew he must be joking—we couldn't be that old already.

A lecture agent somehow heard about the evening. Next thing I knew, I was on the college lecture circuit…

…And drifting back from thoughts of Marquette to find myself under the elm tree in the rain outside Amherst College, ready to hook up to all that energy waiting inside the auditorium to talk about:

The Midnight Express Experience
From Turkey to Hollywood and Beyond

"I couldn't handle Norman's death and deal with the daily demands of prison life, so I buried him. Deep inside myself in this metal box where I crammed all the pain and fear I couldn't face." I was a small figure standing behind a microphone on a distant stage, but my amplified voice carried out over the hushed group. "This metal box was full, and the lid was rattling by the time I escaped. In my normal fashion, I tried to ignore it, hoping it would go away. It doesn't work that way."

My wet Reeboks squished softly on the wooden floor as I shifted back and forth. "There was so much violence and negativity in the air, you couldn't just let it seep in. You built this shield around your emotions. You became hard like a rock or you broke—I don't know which is worse." A damp audience of young, attentive faces stared up from their seats. "After awhile, I could watch the most awful things happen and not be affected. Nothing got in, but nothing got out, either, and when you ignore another human being's pain, it's at a cost to your own humanity."

A question from a girl in the front row who'd been taking notes. "Don't you think it strange that you're made out to be a hero for doing something illegal, smuggling drugs?"

"Yes, I think it's very strange. And I don't know what to say about this hero shit. I'm not proud of the fact that I was arrested and spent five years in prison, or that my family suffered so much pain for what I did. I am proud of the fact that I survived and escaped. Escaping gave me back my self-esteem. In prison, everything around you says that you're a loser, you're a loser, and when you believe that, you are. I was at that point and desperate enough to try anything to get out. The escape was important for me, but it was just getting back to even—I felt like I'd been underwater for five years, and when my head finally broke the surface, the media-gulls were there."

A tall, balding man with a salt and pepper moustache stood up in the front row. We'd been aware of each other from the moment I stepped to the podium. "I am Mehmet Orhan, professor of Middle Eastern Culture here. I am also Turkish." I nodded to the obvious. "I came here tonight not liking Billy Hayes very much. After hearing you speak, I like you a bit more and have sympathy for your family. But I must also speak about the damage this racist film, and it is racist, as you yourself admitted, has done my country."

"Excuse me," I said, "but I didn't say that—I don't want to paint the whole film as racist. I did say that I thought it was unfair to the Turkish people because there were no good Turks in the movie."

"Yes, I know, and I have read your book—a little exaggerated, perhaps, but not the blatant racist attack this movie is."

"Look, everyone involved in the movie-making process must take some responsibility for the final product—some, obviously, more than others. I don't think anyone started out to make all Turks look bad. The intent, certainly by me, and I believe by the filmmakers, was to talk about hope and fear and the human spirit struggling against adversity. We wanted to expose a hypocritical legal system and a brutal prison system. These are things I know about—they should be addressed. But I had Turkish friends in prison, real friends with dignity who would stand by you. So I agree with you about the damage the film may have done to the image of the Turkish people."

"People seeing this movie must think all Turks are animals."

"Yes, and that's obviously not true. You, yourself, being the best example of that. I sympathize with you."

"I believe you do, but the damage is done—millions of people have already seen this movie." He gestured to the seats beside him—a quiet woman and two beautiful dark-eyed children. "My family also suffers now because of it."

"I know."

"And more will see it on TV."

"Yes."

"So what do you say to this?"

"What can I say, other than what I've just said? What I've been saying since the beginning."

"In the courtroom speech you call us a nation of pigs and speak obscenely about our women."

"Yes, the courtroom speech in the movie, which I didn't write. In the book, as you know, I said to the Court that I couldn't agree with them, all I could do...was forgive them."

Mehmet looked at me a moment.

"*Getchmis olsun,*" I offered, in Turkish.

"May it pass quickly for you, also," he said, in English.

Ten hands shot up around the auditorium.

52

Full Circle

March, 1984: I was huddled in the doorway of an old brick building on West 42nd Street in Manhattan when a cold morning drizzle began to fall. Several seedy-looking characters were crammed in beside me. We were waiting for the prison van to pick us up. The van was late, but so were two members of the cast. Our small Off-Off-Broadway theatre was above us, up five flights of stairs. I'd been with these actors almost a year, since Wendy and I had moved back to New York, and I loved being a working member of a theatre company. I was onstage acting and backstage building flats and painting sets. I felt accepted and respected as a dedicated actor.

This was my first chance to direct; we were doing a production of *The Cage*, a powerful and surreal prison play written in San Quentin Prison by Rick Cluchey. For some reason, the company thought I was the right director for this one. It was originally written for men, but we were doing it with a female cast.

Two of the women, shy blonde Brita and street-punk Alexa, were in the doorway with me, along with Surfer Tommy, our slightly loose stage manager. The other two women arrived in a spray of water as a dirty Yellow Cab skittered to a stop in front of us. The cab rocked a bit as Mimi gracefully moved her imposing body onto the street. As always, she was clad in colors, bright contrasts against her dark brown skin. There was arguing inside the cab, then Elizabeth bolted out and slammed the door. The cabbie shouted an obscenity

The Neighborhood Group Theatre
Proudly Presents
The First Female Version of

THE CAGE

BY
RICK CLUCHEY

directed by William Hayes
produced by Kathryn Ballou

Featuring:
Elizabeth Bove*, Maryellen Doumbouya*, Wendy Owen,
Brita Elizabeth Schlosser, Barbara Thomas,
David Wilbur

Opens Friday January 11th
Runs Wednesdays – Saturdays at 8:00 p.m.
Sundays at 2:30 p.m., Limited Run

420 West 42nd Street
Theatre Row
Tickets: $8.00
Call 279-4200 for Reservations

Equity Approved*

and fishtailed away while Liz cranked him the elbow. She stood in the rain a moment glaring at us, then broke into a huge grin. I'd told everyone to come in character, and Liz loved the madwoman/convict she was playing. We were going to Rikers Island Women's House of Detention, where I thought my cast of "convicts" might gain some insights into their characters. This would be my first time back behind prison walls since escaping, so I figured on some interesting insights myself.

I saw a gray van nosing its way up 42nd Street, the old, balding driver straining to see building numbers through the rain-splattered windshield. The woman from the prison had told me on the phone that Leonard would be our driver.

"Yo, Leonard!" I shouted, stepping out to the curb.

Leonard pulled the van over and rolled down the passenger window. "You the actor peoples goin' out to Rikers?" He might have boxed or played football in his younger days and still looked like a rough customer.

"Yeah, that's us," I said.

"Well, load 'em up. Traffic's a bitch in this rain."

I slid open the side door and the crew piled in. Leonard checked us out then turned back in his seat, shaking his head and chuckling. "Boy, this'd be the last place I want to go visit." As we moved out into traffic, I think I was beginning to agree with him.

I remembered the battered red prison van that used to take us from Sagmalcilar Prison, on the outskirts of Istanbul, to the courtroom in the center of the city. It was built to hold fifteen men, but the guards always crammed in thirty or more. We were usually chained at the wrist to another prisoner, which made it difficult to keep your face pressed against the mesh-covered window slats where you watched the world passing by just beyond your outstretched yearning. It also made it quite unpleasant when your chain-partner became motion sick and puked all over himself.

I was snapped out of these pleasant reveries by the sight of Rikers Island looming out of the rain across a long empty causeway. The cast had been goofing around, running lines in character, but now the talking stopped.

When we reached the first checkpoint I looked at the barbed wire atop the high chain link fences. The Women's Building was on the far side of what could have been a deserted college campus. Leonard deposited us at the Visitors Entrance. "I'll meet you right here at four," he said with a smile. "You have a nice day."

Purses and bags were searched. A large black guard named Julius gave me a warm smile and invited me to step through the metal detector. I smiled back and stepped through, a slight tingle of apprehension in the back of my neck. No bells rang, so Julius invited the women to "follow your director." Then Surfer Tommy strolled through with that shiteatin' California-kid grin on his handsome face, and the metal detector went off like a goosed pinball machine. Tommy let out a large laugh, totally amused by the ringing sound as Julius took a step toward him.

"Would you please step back through here, sir? Are you wearing a belt?"

"Oh, yeah, my garrison belt," said Tommy, hauling up his sweatshirt and removing the big leather belt. The tingling sensation in my neck had spread down my spine. Tommy stepped through the metal detector and set it off again. He was surprised this time but he wasn't laughing. I found myself edging away from the group, feeling around for a wall to press my back against. Julius asked him to empty his pockets. When the machine went off again, Julius took Tommy aside and scanned him with a hand detector. He found a small screwdriver in the knee-pocket of Tommy's overalls.

"Wow, Dude," said Tommy, "I *totally* forgot that was there." Julius stared at him. "I'm the stage manager. I'm always fixing things...you know?" Julius stared a moment longer, then nodded to another guard behind a plate glass window. The sudden clatter of machinery startled me as the gray bar door slid open and Julius motioned for us to enter.

A stout matron greeted us on the other side. I was shaking her hand when the door clanged shut behind me. A shiver ran through my body. "This the first time you all been Inside?" she asked the group, her eyes never leaving my face. A few murmured responses. I said nothing, having automatically slipped into the null-info prison mode I knew so well. She smiled at me. "My name is Mrs. Ruiz and I'm your guide today." A double line of women in drab green smocks marched past us, with curious glances from both directions. Surfer Tommy and I received some special attention.

"You guys are the actors, right? " said Mrs. Ruiz, leading us down what could have been a school hallway, except for the barred windows. "I'll show you around some of the cells and workshops, but mostly we'll be in the day room where you can talk to the inmates. I'd like you to stay together and not wander off, especially our two handsome caballeros."

Liz goosed me and I let out a squeal. "Relax," she whispered. "You're just visiting today...*visiting.*"

I tried to remember that, but there were alarms ringing in my nervous system, and the air seemed a bit too thick to breathe. We moved along a row of small, clean, well-lit cells. They were similar in set-up, with a bed, fold-down desk and chair, and toilet facilities in the rear, but each had been personalized according to the taste and means of the current occupant. Some of the women prisoners spoke with us, asked or answered questions, but most ignored us or glared back until we'd passed their cell.

When we came to an unoccupied cell, Mrs. Ruiz invited the cast to step in and look around. It was crowded with five of them in there, so I stayed out in the hall, took a few deep breaths and tried to relax the tight muscles in my shoulders. I turned around to find a young Latino woman staring at me from the edge of her bunk. She took a long, slow drag off her cigarette and let her eyes move along my body. She blew the smoke out toward me, and I felt myself becoming aroused. We looked at each other a moment, then Mrs. Ruiz tapped me on the shoulder. I quickly spun around. The cast was smiling at me. The cell was empty.

"Don't you want to go in?" asked Alexa. "See what it feels like?"

I really didn't want to enter that little room, and I already knew what it felt like, but it was too late to back down now.

Five paces from the cell door to the far wall. Pivot, spin, then back to the bars. Pivot, spin, back to the wall. I fell into the familiar rhythm with an unsettling ease. Then I lay on the bunk and closed my eyes. Muffled voices and distant sounds of metal clanging in concrete walls. Once again the thought: Suppose I'm still in Istanbul and the last ten years have just been a dream? I thought I heard someone speaking to me in Turkish and bolted upright on the bed.

"William?" said Mrs. Ruiz, "William? You look very comfortable there, but we have to move on." Move on, indeed.

There were a dozen women scattered about the day room, sitting in worn Naugahyde chairs, watching TV or playing cards on a folding table. They all looked up as we entered.

"Well, lookee here," said a black woman with patches of short stubbly hair on her almost bald head. "Visitors."

"Yes, Sherry, visitors," said Mrs. Ruiz, "so you treat 'em nice." They stared at each other. "These ladies are actors, doing a play about prison, so maybe you can talk to them. They've agreed to come back out here next month and give a performance—so you be nice, you hear?"

Sherry ignored her and stared at blonde Brita.

"I'll be back in an hour," Mrs. Ruiz told me, "or you call the guard station if you need anything." There was an awkward silence after she left. The actors looked at the prisoners, the prisoners looked at the actors, while a soap opera droned over the TV set mounted high up on the wall.

"Actors, huh?" said Sherry, rising and slowly circling Brita. "So what you want out here? You want to *study us*, see how the animals live?" Brita flinched when Sherry reached up to touch her blonde locks. "Then go out to the fuckin' zoo! Ain't nobody here wants to talk to you."

Brita seemed a little shaken. This is great, thought the director in me, since her character in the play is an innocent thrown in among hardened convicts. But Big Mimi's character was no innocent, and she was having none of this intimidation bullshit.

"No need to talk like that, Sherry. My name's Mimi, and we just trying to find out what it's like here so we can do justice to the play."

"Well, *Mimi*, stay here a couple of years, talk to me then about justice."

Some of the other women seemed curious about us, but Sherry was obviously running the show. She looked at Tommy and me. "And you two *cabrons*, you gettin' off being around all these caged women?"

"Oh, yeah, this is intense to the max," said Tommy, his smiling sincerity lost on Sherry.

"Tommy's the stage manager," I said, "and I'm directing this play because I spent some time in prison. So I can appreciate how you feel."

"You can, huh?" Sherry looked me over and smirked. "Yeah, I bet you had a *real* good time in jail."

I could see this approach wasn't working. The soap opera on TV was *All My Children*, a show I'd been on a few times doing small parts. "I'm also an actor. I see you ladies are watching my show."

"What'd you mean, your show?" asked the only white prisoner, a thin, pale girl with bad skin.

"I've done some small roles on it, that's all."

"No shit?" asked Sherry, her opinion of me changing.

"Yeah, I was the saxophone player in the band when Erica got married on that yacht."

"I saw that one!" cried the white girl, "when they were all dressed up so fine and the killer shot the groom during the ceremony."

"I was on the show once, too," piped Alexa. "I played a hooker in 'the Goalpost.'" The ice was broken. The women gathered around, and soon everyone was talking. Once again the soaps prove to be a common denominator of communication.

"The worst thing about prison," said Sherry in response to a question from Mimi, "ain't the conditions here. I lived in worst places on the Outside. And it ain't a lack of men. Who the fuck needs 'em?" She smiled at Brita. "Hell, we get along fine without men." Sherry's smile faded. "The worst part is if you have a kid, not knowin' how your baby is, not having 'em there to hug or smell when you wake up every morning. That's what tears my heart."

"And the time," said Marlene, the skinny white girl. "Eight months I done here and another six before I get out. I'm twenty-three. These are supposed to be my best years, right? I'm losing my looks. How am I supposed to make it Outside when my looks are gone?"

I remembered the dull ache each look in a mirror would bring—as the years of prison slowly eroded my face and rotted the teeth from my head.

"Shit, girl," said Sherry, "you look better now than when you came in here. That junk you used to shoot Outside fuck you up faster than jail ever will."

"There a lot of drugs in here?" asked Alexa, whose character was supposed to be a junkie.

Sherry eyed her suspiciously. "No, sugar, there ain't no drugs in here. That would be illegal."

"How about crazy people?" asked Liz, whose character has gone insane after eighteen years behind the walls. "What if somebody really goes nuts?"

"Honey, you got to be crazy just to stand this place. But if you *really* flip out, they ship you to Bellevue. I been there once. Them locked wards at Bellevue at night are *not* where you want to be, believe me."

Time flowed by. The women spoke intimately to each other—the prisoners sensing the actors' empathy. I mostly observed and absorbed, balancing the present moment with past memories. When Mrs. Ruiz returned, there were embraces and shared promises to write. They said they'd look for us in May when we'd come back out with the show.

Later, the prison performance was canceled after Rikers officials saw the show in New York—"potentially disruptive," they called it. I don't think any of the actresses ever wrote letters to the prisoners. That's okay, I understood. But the connections they made at Rikers did something for their performances, gave them another level of awareness that reached the audience each evening.

We were subdued in the van leaving the prison. Leonard noticed our mood. "We're worn out," said Liz.

"The place'll do that to you," nodded Leonard.

There's a bittersweet nature to prison visits—both for those who leave and those who stay behind. A vague, empty space opened within me as I balanced the moment with the memory of my hollow feeling as I walked back to my cellblock while my visitor returned to the Outside world. Only this time I was the one who was leaving. I was building a life that I wouldn't need to escape from, and there was someone waiting at home who loved me.

———

ABOUT THE AUTHOR

Billy Hayes has been writing, speaking, acting, and directing in theater, film, and television since his escape in 1975. He lives with his wife, Wendy, in Los Angeles, still practices yoga daily, and appreciates every sweet, magical moment.

For more information, please go to www.billyhayes.com.